THE COMPLETE
CUISINART
AIR FRYER
OVEN COOKBOOK

The Easy and Delicious Air Fryer Recipes
for Your Cuisinart Air Fryer Toaster
Oven on A Budget

Jonathan S. Gibson

#2021

Legal & Disclaimer

The information contained in this book and its contents is not designed to replace or take the place of any form of medical or professional advice; and is not meant to replace the need for independent medical, financial, legal or other professional advice or services, as may be required. The content and information in this book has been provided for educational and entertainment purposes only.

The content and information contained in this book has been compiled from sources deemed reliable, and it is accurate to the best of the Author's knowledge, information and belief. However, the Author cannot guarantee its accuracy and validity and cannot be held liable for any errors and/or omissions. Further, changes are periodically made to this book as and when needed. Where appropriate and/or necessary, you must consult a professional (including but not limited to your doctor, attorney, financial advisor or such other professional advisor) before using any of the suggested remedies, techniques, or information in this book.

CONTENT

Part I introduction

Part II The Recipe

Introduction

With a rise in popularity over the last decade, air fryers have been in the spotlight for their ability to quickly give your food a crispy taste without the use of oil and other additional fat. It is the healthy alternative to deep frying, and it is a cooking method that takes very little time when you compare it to most others. As quickly as you can microwave a meal, you can also use your air fryer to give the ingredients a more gourmet feel. The Cuisinart TOA-6o model is an air fryer and toaster oven in one. Because it does so much, many people are quick to say that it is their favorite model on the market -even Oprah!

Structurally, the appliance is sturdy and sleek. It contains a simple control panel of four knobs. There is a window that looks into the main oven so you can see exactly how crisp your food is getting. Below is the crumb-catcher, which makes for easy clean-up when you are finished cooking. It measures 14" by 15.8" by 14". This allows it to fit on almost any countertop surface that you have in your kitchen. Not much bigger than a standard toaster oven, it comes with many additional perks.

The dials control the appliance's functions, and they are easy to master. First is the timer. This standard control allows you to choose your length of cooking time. By selecting On," you are telling the oven to stay on for 60 minutes. It will shut off on its own after this time. The temperature dial ranges between 250-450 degrees Fahrenheit. With the function dial, you are able to select the mode of the device. You can broil, bake, toast, and air fry. The final dial is another timer that is similar to the first, though with this other timer, the main difference is that it is a quicker setting if you intend on doing something simple--like toasting bread. All you need to do is select your toast shade, and the oven will turn off automatically after your toast is done.

This unit features a crumb tray that can also be used as a baking pan, oven rack, and fryer basket. Because this is something that already comes with your Cuisinart TOA- -60, you don't need to worry about purchasing many additional accessories for it to function the way you need it to. An important note is that none of the accessories that come with this model are dishwasher safe, so you will need to make sure you are properly washing them by hand to keep them in pristine condition. For the number of pros that you get, these are sure to outweigh the few cons.

You are going to love your Cuisinart TOA-60 because of its notable versatility. Whether you want to fry chicken wings or bake a pizza, this device can do it all. With more functionality than most other air fryers you will find on the market, you won't need to make separate purchases to cook all the recipes that you love. It feels great to know that your unit is capable of cooking everything that you crave without having to rely on any other appliances for help. Plus, its great design will leave you feeling confident every time you use it. The stainless steel exterior shell looks great in every kitchen, and it has a simple design that will remain timeless for countless years to come.

What Are the Advantages?

When you are cooking for a family, you need a device that has a larger capacity—the Cuisinart TOA-60 is the device for you. It is larger than your standard air fryer or toaster oven without taking up too much extra space on your countertop. You will easily be able to cook meals that are meant to be eaten by multiple people without having to put in a lot of extra time or effort. This is one of the TOA-60's biggest advantages, and many users agree that this makes it very enjoyable to use. Even if you do not have a large family to feed, being able to cook up bigger batches of food will save you a lot of time that you no longer need to spend in the kitchen. You already have a busy schedule, so it helps to be able to make the most of your free time.

Because this device is multi-functional, it eliminates the need for you to have a separate air fryer and toaster oven. It is a 2-in-1 that will end up saving you money. Even if your budget isn't tight, it makes sense to save as much money as possible with the rising costs of food and other appliances like this on the market. You can expect to pay anywhere between $150-$200 for the TOA-60, and this becomes a very worthy investment that ends up paying for itself over time.

Nothing is worse than a cluttered countertop. It can become cumbersome when you have too many appliances to choose from. When you want to fry, bake, toast, or broil, you won't have to get out any additional appliances from your cupboards. The Cuisinart TOA-60 fits neatly on your kitchen countertop, and it still leaves plenty of room for the rest of your appliances and kitchen items. Since it isn't an eyesore, you will feel great about keeping it out all the time. Plus, having easy access to it will encourage you to use it more often.

When you are cooking in large batches, one big problem that you encounter is unevenness in the final result. Even putting a large batch of veggies in the oven might result in some being well done while other pieces are undercooked. The air fryer element of the Cuisinart TOA-60 eliminates this problem for you. With this device, you get even cooking every time. There is also no need to flip anything or adjust anything—all you need to do is put your ingredients inside and set the dials; it doesn't get any easier than this.

You are going to become a more efficient cook when you use your Cuisinart TOA-60. Because you do not have to constantly stand around to monitor if your food is going to burn or overcook, you can go about your day without any worries. It is a controlled method for cooking that offers you great results every time. Since it is a lot faster than a conventional oven, you won't have to spend as much time preparing to make your meals.

Unboxing and Setup Made Easy

As you are figuring out where to place your Cuisinart TOA-60, you need to make sure that you have at least two to four inches of space on all sides of it to provide proper ventilation. Make sure that it is not resting on top of any sensitive surfaces that will show discoloration or get too hot. Be sure that you do not store any accessories or other objects on top of the air fryer, as they have the potential to overheat. The only thing that you need to do to begin using your air fryer is plug it into the wall. After double-checking that the crumb tray is in place, you can start cooking.

If you plan on broiling foods, it is recommended that you use the air fryer basket placed on top of the baking pan in the second position on the rack. This will give you the most even cooking coverage. You can use the same setup if you want to bake in your air fryer, switching rack positions depending on how much heat you need. Most larger items, like chicken and other baked goods, will need to be moved to the first rack position to allow them ample room to heat. When you are air frying, you can place the basket onto the baking pan and leave the rack in position two.

It is never mandatory to add any oils to your air fryer, although some people do to enhance the flavors of the ingredients. With your Cuisinart TOA-60, you will be able to create crisp results without needing to add any messy or fattening oils. For most batches that you air fry, there is no need to flip or toss the food. You can simply leave it cooking for the duration of the time you select. If you do happen to load the basket until it is very full, you can flip the ingredients halfway through to ensure that they will be evenly cooked.

You can coat your food many different ways to give it the crisp texture that you desire. Many people enjoy using breadcrumbs or panko to get a nice crust. You can also opt for alternatives such as cornflakes, potato chip breadcrumbs, graham cracker crumbs, quinoa, and various flours. With so much versatility and the lack of need for any oil, you will be able to create many delicious recipes without having to worry about putting in any extra effort or cooking time.

Cooking Tips for All Chefs

Using the table below that is provided by Cuisinart, you now have access to a quick and easy guide to follow as you cook various meals:

Food	Recommended Amount	Temperature	Time
Bacon	Eight Slices	400-degrees F	Eight to 10 Minutes
Chicken Wings	Three Pounds	400-degrees F	20-25 Minutes
Frozen Appetizers (mozzarella sticks, corn dogs, popcorn shrimp, etc...)	One and a Half Pounds	400-degrees F	Five to Seven Minutes
Frozen Chicken Nuggets	About 34	400-degrees F	10 Minutes
Frozen Fish Sticks	About 20	400-degrees F	Eight Minutes
Frozen Fries	One to Two Pounds	450-degrees F	15-25 Minutes
Frozen Steak Fries	One to Two Pounds	450-degrees F	15-25 Minutes
Hand-Cut Fries	Two Pounds	400-degrees F	15-20 Minutes
Hand-Cut Steak Fries	Two Pounds	400-degrees F	15-20 Minutes
Shrimp	One Pound	375-degrees F	Eight to 10 Minutes
Tortilla Chips	Six Tortillas	400-degrees F	Five to Six Minutes, Tossing Halfway Through

While a lot of these cooking times can be left up to personal preference, this table will help to give you a basic idea of how fast you can expect your Cuisinart TOA-60 to cook your food. As seen, it is a much faster alternative to a conventional oven, and it won't heat up your entire house in the process. This is great for those warmer months when you don't want to add any extra heat to the room. Based on the items and times you see above, you should be able to get a basic idea of how to cook many different meals and ingredients. The best way to learn how to use your Cuisinart TOA-60 is by using it often.

Cleaning and Care: The Essentials

Knowing how to clean your Cuisinart TOA-60 is important because it will last longer the better you take care of it. As mentioned, its components are not dishwasher friendly, so make sure that you are thoroughly hand-washing these accessories. Keep an eye on your crumb tray—this should be emptied before each use. If you proceed to cook with crumbs in the tray, they can start to burn up and impact the taste of your food and the safety of your air fryer. After waiting until the device is cool, you can easily remove the crumb tray and wipe it down with a warm, soapy sponge. The effort required to clean your air fryer is very minimal, which is great for those who are busy or on the go all the time.

For the exterior of your air fryer, you don't need to be too concerned about cleaning it daily. A regularly weekly dusting of its surface will do just fine. As mentioned, be sure that you are not blocking any of the ventilation slots that are located on the sides of the unit. If you do, then you might be jeopardizing your meals and the items on the countertop around the device. It is always best to give your air fryer a little extra space as a safety precaution. Without anything in the vicinity nearby, you won't have to worry about potential fires or other hazards.

When you are doing any type of internal cleaning of the machine, it is necessary to wait until it cools down, and it is also a good idea to unplug it from the electrical outlet. This will guarantee your safety as you move the various pieces around to clean them. Do not use anything too abrasive, such as wire sponges or cleaners with harsh chemicals like ammonia. They can damage the inside of your Cuisinart air fryer, and you will also be ingesting these chemicals the next time you cook. This is why warm, soapy water and a regular sponge is always the preferred method of cleaning for your air fryer.

For tough food residue, you can switch to a damp cleaning cloth. The warmth should be able to break down these particles to give your Cuisinart a thorough cleaning. The good news is that you do not need to dismantle anything to get your air fryer properly cleaned. Each element of the air fryer comes out easily and can be put back inside just as easily. This saves you from the hassle of dealing with any complicated assembly. Also, you do not necessarily have to wipe down your Cuisinart after every single use. To determine when to clean it, use your best judgment. Keep an eye on any build-up that starts to form. If you smell any type of burning while cooking, this is a sign that you probably have some food residue to clean from the inner walls or the crumb tray.

Though you probably won't be using any oils, grease can still build up inside of your unit. Make sure you are using a dish soap that can power through grease, leaving your Cuisinart free of any remaining grease residue. You will be able to feel the grease as you are cleaning it, and you might have to wipe it down a few times to completely get rid of the slickness. Overall, it is not a complex process. Many users love how easy it is to clean because it is more time efficient than doing dishes after using a deep fryer or frying pan.

A Comparison: Cuisinart TOA-60 vs. Cuisinart ARF-25

To make the best choice when it comes to the air fryer you purchase, let's take a look at another similar model that you might want to consider. The ARF-25 has some different features when compared to the TOA-60. The table below will inform you about their differences, pros, and cons.

Model	Cuisinart TOA-60	Cuisinart ARF-25
Overview	This model is a great air fryer/toaster oven with many capabilities. You can cook for your entire family with one device. It is equally easy to use as it is to clean. Larger than a standard toaster oven, it still fits nicely on a standard kitchen countertop.	This air fryer is more compact, but it comes with a noticeably larger depth capacity. It is around half the price of the TOA-60, if you are on a budget and are looking for something cheaper. The interface is simpler, it only contains two dials used for temperature and time. It only has the ability to air fry, unless you place the food on a low heat setting for a longer amount of time.
Pros	• Versatility (air fryer and toaster oven combo) • Beautiful Design • Efficient Oven Performance • Great Size • Ease of Use • Three-Year Warranty	• A Less Expensive Option • More Compact on Your Countertop • A Great and Simple Air Fryer That Does Not Require Oil • Easy to Clean Without Much Food Residue Sticking to the Inside
Cons	• Timer is Sometimes Not Precise • Food Does Require Turning When Cooked in Large Batches • Accessories Are Not Dishwasher Friendly	• No Presets to Use for Other Types of Cooking • Cannot Toast as Easily as the TOA-60 • Not Dishwasher Safe • Designed for Cooking in Smaller Batches Than the TOA-60

It is important to compare the differences between the Cuisinart TOA-60 and at least one other model on the market. You need to make sure you are getting the best unit for your needs. As you can see, the two are very similar in upholding the quality that Cuisinart air fryers promise. The main difference is that the TOA-60 has more functions, and it is bigger than the ARF-25. If you live alone or will only be preparing small batches of food, the ARF-25 can be a great option for you, though it is not as highly recommended as the TOA-60. You can always cut down your portion size while using an air fryer, but you cannot cook more if the device does not have enough room.

Though the ARF-25 is around half the price, it still could likely be worthwhile to purchase the TOA-60 because of all the added benefits you get. The air fryer ends up paying for itself over time, and it is so easy and functional to use. Because you get so many different setting controls, you will be able to customize your recipes to your liking. Even when you want to warm up a few quick appetizers for a get-together, the TOA-60 will be able to do this for you without any problems.

Depending on the type of cooking you will be doing and the number of people you will be feeding, the table above can serve as your guide as to which model is the better decision for you. Of course, this is all based on personal preference. Doing your research will lead you to the best conclusion possible about which air fryer to purchase. Overall, both of these models are going to be of great quality because that is the standard that Cuisinart represents. Either way, you will not be disappointed with the results you see.

About the Recipes—Endless Possibilities

After becoming more familiar with the Cuisinart TOA-60 and all that it can do, you probably can't wait to get into the kitchen. There are 150 recipes in this cookbook that you are going to love. Based on the skill level of a beginner chef, you should have no problem prepping and cooking these meals. Before long, you will have a long list of favorites that you revisit frequently. The great thing about all of these recipes is that they are designed to be versatile. We provide you with a base list of ingredients and cooking instructions, but you do not have to stick to them precisely. When you become more comfortable with your Cuisinart, you will be able to use any of these recipes as a foundation for one that you create to your own specifications and preferences.

Most of the ingredients provided in the recipes can be substituted for your liking. Think about them as suggestions rather than concrete choices. This helps tremendously if you are cooking for picky eaters, those with food allergies, or anyone who might be particular about the food that they are eating. Making substitutions makes cooking fun, and it allows you to feel that you are more involved in the creative process of coming up with recipes. Overall, cooking should feel fun. It should not be something that you dread doing, and your Cuisinart TOA-60 will show you just how enjoyable it can be.

You won't even feel like you are cooking most of the time because of how little time you will be required to stand around in the kitchen. Once you prepare the food, the Cuisinart will take over to do the rest. You can rest assured that your end result is going to be amazing and delicious. The worst part of cooking is always the clean-up, but your TOA-60 will also simplify this process for you. Being able to wipe down a few surfaces is a lot better than spending an hour over the kitchen sink after you are full and happy.

Keep in mind that a lot of your standard recipes can be converted into air fryer recipes. If you are used to making homemade french fries in the deep fryer, you can easily substitute that device for your Cuisinart air fryer. With no oil involved, your fries just got a lot easier to make. Even delicacies such as quiches, casseroles, and other baked goods can be created in your TOA-60 without the need to turn the conventional oven on. The great part is, you might not even have to wait for hours before you can enjoy your food. Air frying technology allows you to get the crisp result without having to wait very long at all.

As you read through each recipe, take note of the ones that sound the best to you. It is helpful to create your own personal collection of go-to recipes so that you can cook a meal in no time at all. When your whole family is hungry and waiting, you need to think quickly. This cookbook is meant to give you several different ideas and meal solutions so you don't have to spend hours doing research. When you can all agree on the ingredients that you love, you should be able to find countless recipes that your Cuisinart TOA-60 is more than capable of creating.

Chapter 1 Breakfasts

Breakfast Cheese Sandwiches

Prep time: 5 minutes | Cook time: 8 minutes | Serves 2

- 1 teaspoon butter, softened
- 4 slices bread
- 4 slices smoked country ham
- 4 slices Cheddar cheese
- 4 thick slices tomato

1. Spoon ½ teaspoon of butter onto one side of 2 slices of bread and spread it all over.
2. Assemble the sandwiches: Top each of 2 slices of unbuttered bread with 2 slices of ham, 2 slices of cheese, and 2 slices of tomato. Place the remaining 2 slices of bread on top, butter-side up.
3. Lay the sandwiches in the baking pan, buttered side down.
4. Slide the baking pan into Rack Position 1, select Convection Bake, set temperature to 370ºF (188ºC), and set time to 8 minutes.
5. Flip the sandwiches halfway through the cooking time.
6. When cooking is complete, the sandwiches should be golden brown on both sides and the cheese should be melted. Remove from the oven. Allow to cool for 5 minutes before slicing to serve.

Ham and Cheese Toast

Prep time: 5 minutes | Cook time: 6 minutes | Serves: 1

- 1 slice bread
- 1 teaspoon butter, at room temperature
- 1 egg
- Salt and freshly ground black pepper, to taste
- 2 teaspoons diced ham
- 1 tablespoon grated Cheddar cheese

1. On a clean work surface, use a 2½-inch biscuit cutter to make a hole in the center of the bread slice with about ½-inch of bread remaining.
2. Spread the butter on both sides of the bread slice. Crack the egg into the hole and season with salt and pepper to taste. Transfer the bread to the air fryer basket.
3. Put the air fryer basket on the baking pan and slide into Rack Position 2, select Air Fry, set temperature to 325ºF (163ºC), and set time to 6 minutes.
4. After 5 minutes, remove the pan from the oven. Scatter the cheese and diced ham on top and continue cooking for an additional 1 minute.
5. When cooking is complete, the egg should be set and the cheese should be melted. Remove the toast from the oven to a plate and let cool for 5 minutes before serving.

Fried Cheese Grits

Prep time: 10 minutes | Cook time: 11 minutes | Serves 4

- ⅔ cup instant grits
- 1 teaspoon salt
- 1 teaspoon freshly ground black pepper
- ¾ cup whole or 2% milk
- 3 ounces (85 g) cream cheese, at room temperature
- 1 large egg, beaten
- 1 tablespoon butter, melted
- 1 cup shredded mild Cheddar cheese
- Cooking spray

1. Mix the grits, salt, and black pepper in a large bowl. Add the milk, cream cheese, beaten egg, and melted butter and whisk to combine. Fold in the Cheddar cheese and stir well.
2. Spray the baking pan with cooking spray. Spread the grits mixture into the baking pan.
3. Put the air fryer basket on the baking pan and slide into Rack Position 2, select Air Fry, set temperature to 400ºF (205ºC) and set time to 11 minutes.
4. Stir the mixture halfway through the cooking time.
5. When done, a knife inserted in the center should come out clean.
6. Rest for 5 minutes and serve warm.

Bourbon Vanilla French Toast

Prep time: 15 minutes | Cook time: 6 minutes | Serves 4

- 2 large eggs
- 2 tablespoons water
- ⅔ cup whole or 2% milk
- 1 tablespoon butter, melted
- 2 tablespoons bourbon
- 1 teaspoon vanilla extract
- 8 (1-inch-thick) French bread slices
- Cooking spray

1. Spray the baking pan with cooking spray.
2. Beat the eggs with the water in a shallow bowl until combined. Add the milk, melted butter, bourbon, and vanilla and stir to mix well.
3. Dredge 4 slices of bread in the batter, turning to coat both sides evenly. Transfer the bread slices to the baking pan.
4. Slide the baking pan into Rack Position 1, select Convection Bake, set temperature to 320ºF (160ºC) and set time to 6 minutes.
5. Flip the slices halfway through the cooking time.
6. When cooking is complete, the bread slices should be nicely browned.
7. Remove from the oven to a plate and serve warm.

Easy Buttermilk Biscuits

Prep time: 5 minutes | Cook time: 18 minutes | Makes 16 biscuits

- 2½ cups all-purpose flour
- 1 tablespoon baking powder
- 1 teaspoon kosher salt
- 1 teaspoon sugar
- ½ teaspoon baking soda
- 8 tablespoons (1 stick) unsalted butter, at room temperature
- 1 cup buttermilk, chilled

1. Stir together the flour, baking powder, salt, sugar, and baking powder in a large bowl.
2. Add the butter and stir to mix well. Pour in the buttermilk and stir with a rubber spatula just until incorporated.
3. Place the dough onto a lightly floured surface and roll the dough out to a disk, ½ inch thick. Cut out the biscuits with a 2-inch round cutter and re-roll any scraps until you have 16 biscuits. Arrange the biscuits in the baking pan.
4. Slide the baking pan into Rack Position 1, select Convection Bake, set temperature to 325ºF (163ºC) and set time to 18 minutes.
5. When cooked, the biscuits will be golden brown.
6. Remove from the oven to a plate and serve hot.

Spinach and Bacon Roll-ups

Prep time: 5 minutes | Cook time: 8 to 9 minutes | Serves 4

- 4 flour tortillas (6- or 7-inch size)
- 4 slices Swiss cheese
- 1 cup baby spinach leaves
- 4 slices turkey bacon

Special Equipment:
- 4 toothpicks, soak in water for at least 30 minutes

1. On a clean work surface, top each tortilla with one slice of cheese and ¼ cup of spinach, then tightly roll them up.
2. Wrap each tortilla with a strip of turkey bacon and secure with a toothpick.
3. Arrange the roll-ups in the air fryer basket, leaving space between each roll-up.
4. Put the air fryer basket on the baking pan and slide into Rack Position 2, select Air Fry, set temperature to 390ºF (199ºC), and set time to 8 minutes.
5. After 4 minutes, remove the pan from the oven. Flip the roll-ups with tongs and rearrange them for more even cooking. Return to the oven and continue cooking for another 4 minutes.
6. When cooking is complete, the bacon should be crisp. If necessary, continue cooking for 1 minute more. Remove the pan from the oven. Rest for 5 minutes and remove the toothpicks before serving.

Eggs in Bell Pepper Rings

Prep time: 5 minutes | Cook time: 7 minutes | Serves 4

- 1 large red, yellow, or orange bell pepper, cut into four ¾-inch rings
- 4 eggs
- Salt and freshly ground black pepper, to taste
- 2 teaspoons salsa
- Cooking spray

1. Coat the baking pan lightly with cooking spray.
2. Put 4 bell pepper rings in the prepared baking pan. Crack one egg into each bell pepper ring and sprinkle with salt and pepper. Top each egg with ½ teaspoon of salsa.
3. Put the air fryer basket on the baking pan and slide into Rack Position 2, select Air Fry, set temperature to 350ºF (180ºC) and set time to 7 minutes.
4. When done, the eggs should be cooked to your desired doneness.
5. Remove the rings from the pan to a plate and serve warm.

Asparagus and Cheese Strata

Prep time: 10 minutes | Cook time: 17 minutes | Serves 4

- 6 asparagus spears, cut into 2-inch pieces
- 1 tablespoon water
- 2 slices whole-wheat bread, cut into ½-inch cubes
- 4 eggs
- 3 tablespoons whole milk
- 2 tablespoons chopped flat-leaf
- parsley
- ½ cup grated Havarti or Swiss cheese
- Pinch salt
- Freshly ground black pepper, to taste
- Cooking spray

1. Add the asparagus spears and 1 tablespoon of water in the baking pan.
2. Slide the baking pan into Rack Position 1, select Convection Bake, set temperature to 330ºF (166ºC) and set time to 4 minutes.
3. When cooking is complete, the asparagus spears will be crisp-tender.
4. Remove the asparagus from the pan and drain on paper towels.
5. Spritz the pan with cooking spray. Place the bread and asparagus in the pan.
6. Whisk together the eggs and milk in a medium mixing bowl until creamy. Fold in the parsley, cheese, salt, and pepper and stir to combine. Pour this mixture into the baking pan.
7. Select Bake and set time to 13 minutes. Put the pan back to the oven. When done, the eggs will be set and the top will be lightly browned.
8. Let cool for 5 minutes before slicing and serving.

Cheesy Breakfast Casserole

Prep time: 10 minutes | Cook time: 16 minutes | Serves 4

- 6 slices bacon
- 6 eggs
- Salt and pepper, to taste
- Cooking spray
- ½ cup chopped green bell pepper
- ½ cup chopped onion
- ¾ cup shredded Cheddar cheese

1. Place the bacon in a skillet over medium-high heat and cook each side for about 4 minutes until evenly crisp. Remove from the heat to a paper towel-lined plate to drain. Crumble it into small pieces and set aside.
2. Whisk the eggs with the salt and pepper in a medium bowl.
3. Spritz the baking pan with cooking spray.
4. Place the whisked eggs, crumbled bacon, green bell pepper, and onion in the prepared pan.
5. Slide the baking pan into Rack Position 1, select Convection Bake, set temperature to 400ºF (205ºC) and set time to 8 minutes.
6. After 6 minutes, remove the pan from the oven. Scatter the Cheddar cheese all over. Return the pan to the oven and continue to cook for another 2 minutes.
7. When cooking is complete, let sit for 5 minutes and serve on plates.

Mixed Berry Dutch Baby Pancake

Prep time: 10 minutes | Cook time: 14 minutes | Serves 4

- 1 tablespoon unsalted butter, at room temperature
- 1 egg
- 2 egg whites
- ½ cup 2% milk
- ½ cup whole-wheat pastry flour
- 1 teaspoon pure vanilla extract
- 1 cup sliced fresh strawberries
- ½ cup fresh raspberries
- ½ cup fresh blueberries

1. Grease the baking pan with the butter.
2. Using a hand mixer, beat together the egg, egg whites, milk, pastry flour, and vanilla in a medium mixing bowl until well incorporated.
3. Pour the batter into the pan.
4. Slide the baking pan into Rack Position 1, select Convection Bake, set temperature to 330ºF (166ºC) and set time to 14 minutes.
5. When cooked, the pancake should puff up in the center and the edges should be golden brown
6. Allow the pancake to cool for 5 minutes and serve topped with the berries.

Rice, Shrimp, and Spinach Frittata

Prep time: 15 minutes | Cook time: 16 minutes | Serves 4

- 4 eggs
- Pinch salt
- ½ cup cooked rice
- ½ cup chopped cooked shrimp
- ½ cup baby spinach
- ½ cup grated Monterey Jack cheese
- Nonstick cooking spray

1. Spritz the baking pan with nonstick cooking spray.
2. Whisk the eggs and salt in a small bowl until frothy.
3. Place the cooked rice, shrimp, and baby spinach in the baking pan. Pour in the whisked eggs and scatter the cheese on top.
4. Slide the baking pan into Rack Position 1, select Convection Bake, set temperature to 320ºF (160ºC) and set time to 16 minutes.
5. When cooking is complete, the frittata should be golden and puffy.
6. Let the frittata cool for 5 minutes before slicing to serve.

Veggie Frittata

Prep time: 10 minutes | Cook time: 12 minutes | Serves 4

- ½ cup chopped red bell pepper
- 1/3 cup grated carrot
- 1/3 cup minced onion
- 1 teaspoon olive oil
- 1 egg
- 6 egg whites
- 1/3 cup 2% milk
- 1 tablespoon shredded Parmesan cheese

1. Mix together the red bell pepper, carrot, onion, and olive oil in the baking pan and stir to combine.
2. Slide the baking pan into Rack Position 1, select Convection Bake, set temperature to 350ºF (180ºC) and set time to 12 minutes.
3. After 3 minutes, remove the pan from the oven. Stir the vegetables. Return the pan to the oven and continue cooking.
4. Meantime, whisk together the egg, egg whites, and milk in a medium bowl until creamy.
5. After 3 minutes, remove the pan from the oven. Pour the egg mixture over the top and scatter with the Parmesan cheese. Return the pan to the oven and continue cooking for additional 6 minutes.
6. When cooking is complete, the eggs will be set and the top will be golden around the edges.
7. Allow the frittata to cool for 5 minutes before slicing and serving.

Coconut Brown Rice Porridge with Dates

Prep time: 5 minutes | Cook time: 23 minutes | Serves 1 or 2

- ½ cup cooked brown rice
- 1 cup canned coconut milk
- ¼ cup unsweetened shredded coconut
- ¼ cup packed dark brown sugar
- 4 large Medjool dates, pitted and roughly chopped
- ½ teaspoon kosher salt
- ¼ teaspoon ground cardamom
- Heavy cream, for serving (optional)

1. Place all the ingredients except the heavy cream in the baking pan and stir until blended.
2. Slide the baking pan into Rack Position 1, select Convection Bake, set temperature to 375ºF (190ºC) and set time to 23 minutes.
3. Stir the porridge halfway through the cooking time.
4. When cooked, the porridge will be thick and creamy.
5. Remove from the oven and ladle the porridge into bowls.
6. Serve hot with a drizzle of the cream, if desired.

Spinach, Leek and Cheese Frittata

Prep time: 10 minutes | Cook time: 22 minutes | Serves 2

- 4 large eggs
- 4 ounces (113 g) baby bella mushrooms, chopped
- 1 cup (1 ounce / 28-g) baby spinach, chopped
- ½ cup (2 ounces / 57-g) shredded Cheddar cheese
- ⅓ cup (from 1 large) chopped leek, white part only
- ¼ cup halved grape tomatoes
- 1 tablespoon 2% milk
- ¼ teaspoon dried oregano
- ¼ teaspoon garlic powder
- ½ teaspoon kosher salt
- Freshly ground black pepper, to taste
- Cooking spray

1. Lightly spritz the baking pan with cooking spray.
2. Whisk the eggs in a large bowl until frothy. Add the mushrooms, baby spinach, cheese, leek, tomatoes, milk, oregano, garlic powder, salt, and pepper and stir until well blended. Pour the mixture into the prepared baking pan.
3. Slide the baking pan into Rack Position 1, select Convection Bake, set temperature to 300ºF (150ºC) and set time to 22 minutes.
4. When cooked, the center will be puffed up and the top will be golden brown.
5. Let the frittata cool for 5 minutes before slicing to serve.

Banana and Oat Bread Pudding

Prep time: 10 minutes | Cook time: 16 minutes | Serves 4

- 2 medium ripe bananas, mashed
- ½ cup low-fat milk
- 2 tablespoons maple syrup
- 2 tablespoons peanut butter
- 1 teaspoon vanilla extract
- 1 teaspoon ground cinnamon
- 2 slices whole-grain bread, cut into bite-sized cubes
- ¼ cup quick oats
- Cooking spray

1. Spritz the baking pan lightly with cooking spray.
2. Mix the bananas, milk, maple syrup, peanut butter, vanilla, and cinnamon in a large mixing bowl and stir until well incorporated.
3. Add the bread cubes to the banana mixture and stir until thoroughly coated. Fold in the oats and stir to combine.
4. Transfer the mixture to the baking pan. Wrap the baking pan in aluminum foil.
5. Slide the baking pan into Rack Position 2, select Air Fry, set temperature to 350ºF (180ºC) and set time to 16 minutes.
6. After 10 minutes, remove the pan from the oven. Remove the foil. Return the pan to the oven and continue to cook for another 6 minutes.
7. When done, the pudding should be set.
8. Let the pudding cool for 5 minutes before serving.

Carrot Banana Muffin

Prep time: 10 minutes | Cook time: 20 minutes | Serves 12

- 1½ cups whole-wheat flour
- 1 cup grated carrot
- 1 cup mashed banana
- ½ cup bran
- ½ cup low-fat buttermilk
- 2 tablespoons agave nectar
- 2 teaspoons baking powder
- 1 teaspoon vanilla
- 1 teaspoon baking soda
- ½ teaspoon nutmeg
- Pinch cloves
- 2 egg whites

1. Line a muffin pan with 12 paper liners.
2. In a large bowl, stir together all the ingredients. Mix well, but do not over beat.
3. Scoop the mixture into the muffin cups.
4. Place the muffin pan into Rack Position 1, select Convection Bake, set temperature to 400ºF (205ºC) and set time to 20 minutes.
5. When cooking is complete, remove from the oven and let rest for 5 minutes.
6. Serve warm or at room temperature.

Breakfast Blueberry Cobbler

Prep time: 5 minutes | Cook time: 15 minutes | Serves 4

- ¾ teaspoon baking powder
- ⅓ cup whole-wheat pastry flour
- Dash sea salt
- ⅓ cup unsweetened nondairy milk
- 2 tablespoons maple syrup
- ½ teaspoon vanilla
- Cooking spray
- ½ cup blueberries
- ¼ cup granola
- Nondairy yogurt, for topping (optional)

1. Spritz the baking pan with cooking spray.
2. Mix together the baking powder, flour, and salt in a medium bowl. Add the milk, maple syrup, and vanilla and whisk to combine.
3. Scrape the mixture into the prepared pan. Scatter the blueberries and granola on top.
4. Slide the baking pan into Rack Position 1, select Convection Bake, set temperature to 347ºF (175ºC) and set time to 15 minutes.
5. When done, the top should begin to brown and a knife inserted in the center should come out clean.
6. Let the cobbler cool for 5 minutes and serve with a drizzle of nondairy yogurt.

Maple Walnut Pancake

Prep time: 10 minutes | Cook time: 20 minutes | Serves 4

- 3 tablespoons melted butter, divided
- 1 cup flour
- 2 tablespoons sugar
- 1½ teaspoons baking powder
- ¼ teaspoon salt
- 1 egg, beaten
- ¾ cup milk
- 1 teaspoon pure vanilla extract
- ½ cup roughly chopped walnuts
- Maple syrup or fresh sliced fruit, for serving

1. Grease the baking pan with 1 tablespoon of melted butter.
2. Mix together the flour, sugar, baking powder, and salt in a medium bowl. Add the beaten egg, milk, the remaining 2 tablespoons of melted butter, and vanilla and stir until the batter is sticky but slightly lumpy.
3. Slowly pour the batter into the greased baking pan and scatter with the walnuts.
4. Slide the baking pan into Rack Position 1, select Convection Bake, set temperature to 330ºF (166ºC) and set time to 20 minutes.
5. When cooked, the pancake should be golden brown and cooked through.
6. Let the pancake rest for 5 minutes and serve topped with the maple syrup or fresh fruit, if desired.

Cheesy Hash Brown Casserole

Prep time: 15 minutes | Cook time: 30 minutes | Serves 4

- 3½ cups frozen hash browns, thawed
- 1 teaspoon salt
- 1 teaspoon freshly ground black pepper
- 3 tablespoons butter, melted
- 1 (10.5-ounce / 298-g) can cream
- of chicken soup
- ½ cup sour cream
- 1 cup minced onion
- ½ cup shredded sharp Cheddar cheese
- Cooking spray

1. Put the hash browns in a large bowl and season with salt and black pepper. Add the melted butter, cream of chicken soup, and sour cream and stir until well incorporated. Mix in the minced onion and cheese and stir well.
2. Spray the baking pan with cooking spray.
3. Spread the hash brown mixture evenly into the baking pan.
4. Slide the baking pan into Rack Position 1, select Convection Bake, set temperature to 325ºF (163ºC) and set time to 30 minutes.
5. When cooked, the hash brown mixture will be browned.
6. Cool for 5 minutes before serving.

Olives, Kale, and Pecorino Baked Eggs

Prep time: 5 minutes | Cook time: 11 minutes | Serves 2

- 1 cup roughly chopped kale leaves, stems and center ribs removed
- ¼ cup grated pecorino cheese
- ¼ cup olive oil
- 1 garlic clove, peeled
- 3 tablespoons whole almonds
- Kosher salt and freshly ground black pepper, to taste
- 4 large eggs
- 2 tablespoons heavy cream
- 3 tablespoons chopped pitted mixed olives

1. Place the kale, pecorino, olive oil, garlic, almonds, salt, and pepper in a small blender and blitz until well incorporated.
2. One at a time, crack the eggs in the baking pan. Drizzle the kale pesto on top of the egg whites. Top the yolks with the cream and swirl together the yolks and the pesto.
3. Slide the baking pan into Rack Position 1, select Convection Bake, set temperature to 300ºF (150ºC) and set time to 11 minutes.
4. When cooked, the top should begin to brown and the eggs should be set.
5. Allow the eggs to cool for 5 minutes. Scatter the olives on top and serve warm.

Chapter 2
Vegetable Sides

Balsamic-Glazed Carrots

Prep time: 5 minutes | Cook time: 18 minutes | Serves 3

- 3 medium-size carrots, cut into 2-inch × ½-inch sticks
- 1 tablespoon orange juice
- 2 teaspoons balsamic vinegar
- 1 teaspoon maple syrup
- 1 teaspoon avocado oil
- ½ teaspoon dried rosemary
- ¼ teaspoon sea salt
- ¼ teaspoon lemon zest

1. Put the carrots in the baking pan and sprinkle with the orange juice, balsamic vinegar, maple syrup, avocado oil, rosemary, sea salt, finished by the lemon zest. Toss well.
2. Slide the baking pan into Rack Position 1, select Convection Bake, set temperature to 375ºF (190ºC), and set time to 18 minutes.
3. Stir the carrots several times during the cooking process.
4. When cooking is complete, the carrots should be nicely glazed and tender. Remove from the oven and serve hot.

Chili Corn on the Cob

Prep time: 10 minutes | Cook time: 15 minutes | Serves 4

- 2 tablespoon olive oil, divided
- 2 tablespoons grated Parmesan cheese
- 1 teaspoon garlic powder
- 1 teaspoon chili powder
- 1 teaspoon ground cumin
- 1 teaspoon paprika
- 1 teaspoon salt
- ¼ teaspoon cayenne pepper (optional)
- 4 ears fresh corn, shucked

1. Grease the air fryer basket with 1 tablespoon of olive oil. Set aside.
2. Combine the Parmesan cheese, garlic powder, chili powder, cumin, paprika, salt, and cayenne pepper (if desired) in a small bowl and stir to mix well.
3. Lightly coat the ears of corn with the remaining 1 tablespoon of olive oil. Rub the cheese mixture all over the ears of corn until completely coated.
4. Arrange the ears of corn in the greased basket in a single layer.
5. Put the air fryer basket on the baking pan and slide into Rack Position 2, select Air Fry, set temperature to 400ºF (205ºC), and set time to 15 minutes.
6. Flip the ears of corn halfway through the cooking time.
7. When cooking is complete, they should be lightly browned. Remove from the oven and let them cool for 5 minutes before serving.

Baked Potatoes with Yogurt and Chives

Prep time: 5 minutes | Cook time: 35 minutes | Serves 4

- 4 (7-ounce / 198-g) russet potatoes, rinsed
- Olive oil spray
- ½ teaspoon kosher salt, divided
- ½ cup 2% plain Greek yogurt
- ¼ cup minced fresh chives
- Freshly ground black pepper, to taste

1. Pat the potatoes dry and pierce them all over with a fork. Spritz the potatoes with olive oil spray. Sprinkle with ¼ teaspoon of the salt.
2. Transfer the potatoes to the baking pan.
3. Slide the baking pan into Rack Position 1, select Convection Bake, set temperature to 400ºF (205ºC), and set time to 35 minutes.
4. When cooking is complete, the potatoes should be fork-tender. Remove from the oven and split open the potatoes. Top with the yogurt, chives, the remaining ¼ teaspoon of salt, and finish with the black pepper. Serve immediately.

Charred Green Beans with Sesame Seeds

Prep time: 5 minutes | Cook time: 8 minutes | Serves 4

- 1 tablespoon reduced-sodium soy sauce or tamari
- ½ tablespoon Sriracha sauce
- 4 teaspoons toasted sesame oil, divided
- 12 ounces (340 g) trimmed green beans
- ½ tablespoon toasted sesame seeds

1. Whisk together the soy sauce, Sriracha sauce, and 1 teaspoon of sesame oil in a small bowl until smooth. Set aside.
2. Toss the green beans with the remaining sesame oil in a large bowl until evenly coated.
3. Place the green beans in the air fryer basket in a single layer.
4. Put the air fryer basket on the baking pan and slide into Rack Position 2, select Air Fry, set temperature to 375ºF (190ºC), and set time to 8 minutes.
5. Stir the green beans halfway through the cooking time.
6. When cooking is complete, the green beans should be lightly charred and tender. Remove from the oven to a platter. Pour the prepared sauce over the top of green beans and toss well. Serve sprinkled with the toasted sesame seeds.

Buttered Broccoli with Parmesan

Prep time: 5 minutes | Cook time: 4 minutes | Serves 4

- 1 pound (454 g) broccoli florets
- 1 medium shallot, minced
- 2 tablespoons olive oil
- 2 tablespoons unsalted butter,
- melted
- 2 teaspoons minced garlic
- ¼ cup grated Parmesan cheese

1. Combine the broccoli florets with the shallot, olive oil, butter, garlic, and Parmesan cheese in a medium bowl and toss until the broccoli florets are thoroughly coated.
2. Place the broccoli florets in the baking pan in a single layer.
3. Slide the baking pan into Rack Position 1, select Convection Bake, set temperature to 350ºF (180ºC), and set time to 4 minutes.
4. When cooking is complete, the broccoli florets should be crisp-tender. Remove from the oven and serve warm.

Creamy Corn Casserole

Prep time: 5 minutes | Cook time: 15 minutes | Serves 4

- 2 cups frozen yellow corn
- 1 egg, beaten
- 3 tablespoons flour
- ½ cup grated Swiss or Havarti cheese
- ½ cup light cream
- ¼ cup milk
- Pinch salt
- Freshly ground black pepper, to taste
- 2 tablespoons butter, cut into cubes
- Nonstick cooking spray

1. Spritz the baking pan with nonstick cooking spray.
2. Stir together the remaining ingredients except the butter in a medium bowl until well incorporated. Transfer the mixture to the prepared baking pan and scatter with the butter cubes.
3. Slide the baking pan into Rack Position 1, select Convection Bake, set temperature to 320ºF (160ºC), and set time to 15 minutes.
4. When cooking is complete, the top should be golden brown and a toothpick inserted in the center should come out clean. Remove from the oven. Let the casserole cool for 5 minutes before slicing into wedges and serving.

Parmesan Asparagus Fries

Prep time: 15 minutes | Cook time: 6 minutes | Serves 4

- 2 egg whites
- ¼ cup water
- ¼ cup plus 2 tablespoons grated Parmesan cheese, divided
- ¾ cup panko bread crumbs
- ¼ teaspoon salt
- 12 ounces (340 g) fresh asparagus spears, woody ends trimmed
- Cooking spray

1. In a shallow dish, whisk together the egg whites and water until slightly foamy. In a separate shallow dish, thoroughly combine ¼ cup of Parmesan cheese, bread crumbs, and salt.
2. Dip the asparagus in the egg white, then roll in the cheese mixture to coat well.
3. Place the asparagus in the air fryer basket in a single layer, leaving space between each spear. Spritz the asparagus with cooking spray.
4. Put the air fryer basket on the baking pan and slide into Rack Position 2, select Air Fry, set temperature to 390ºF (199ºC), and set time to 6 minutes.
5. When cooking is complete, the asparagus should be golden brown and crisp. Remove from the oven. Sprinkle with the remaining 2 tablespoons of cheese and serve hot.

Cinnamon-Spiced Acorn Squash

Prep time: 5 minutes | Cook time: 15 minutes | Serves 2

- 1 medium acorn squash, halved crosswise and deseeded
- 1 teaspoon coconut oil
- 1 teaspoon light brown sugar
- Few dashes of ground cinnamon
- Few dashes of ground nutmeg

1. On a clean work surface, rub the cut sides of the acorn squash with coconut oil. Scatter with the brown sugar, cinnamon, and nutmeg.
2. Put the squash halves in the air fryer basket, cut-side up.
3. Put the air fryer basket on the baking pan and slide into Rack Position 2, select Air Fry, set temperature to 325ºF (163ºC), and set time to 15 minutes.
4. When cooking is complete, the squash halves should be just tender when pierced in the center with a paring knife. Remove from the oven. Rest for 5 to 10 minutes and serve warm.

Garlic Asparagus

Prep time: 5 minutes | Cook time: 10 minutes | Serves 4

- 1 pound (454 g) asparagus, woody ends trimmed
- 2 tablespoons olive oil
- 1 tablespoon balsamic vinegar
- 2 teaspoons minced garlic
- Salt and freshly ground black pepper, to taste

1. In a large shallow bowl, toss the asparagus with the olive oil, balsamic vinegar, garlic, salt, and pepper until thoroughly coated. Put the asparagus in the baking pan.
2. Slide the baking pan into Rack Position 1, select Convection Bake, set temperature to 350ºF (180ºC), and set time to 10 minutes.
3. Flip the asparagus with tongs halfway through the cooking time.
4. When cooking is complete, the asparagus should be crispy. Remove from the oven and serve warm.

Spicy Broccoli with Hot Sauce

Prep time: 5 minutes | Cook time: 14 minutes | Serves 6

Broccoli:
- 1 medium-sized head broccoli, cut into florets
- 1½ tablespoons olive oil
- 1 teaspoon shallot powder
- 1 teaspoon porcini powder
- ½ teaspoon freshly grated lemon zest
- ½ teaspoon hot paprika
- ½ teaspoon granulated garlic
- $1/3$ teaspoon fine sea salt
- $1/3$ teaspoon celery seeds

Hot Sauce:
- ½ cup tomato sauce
- 1 tablespoon balsamic vinegar
- ½ teaspoon ground allspice

1. In a mixing bowl, combine all the ingredients for the broccoli and toss to coat. Transfer the broccoli to the air fryer basket.
2. Put the air fryer basket on the baking pan and slide into Rack Position 2, select Air Fry, set temperature to 360ºF (182ºC), and set time to 14 minutes.
3. Meanwhile, make the hot sauce by whisking together the tomato sauce, balsamic vinegar, and allspice in a small bowl.
4. When cooking is complete, remove the broccoli from the oven and serve with the hot sauce.

Spicy Cabbage

Prep time: 5 minutes | Cook time: 7 minutes | Serves 4

- 1 head cabbage, sliced into 1-inch-thick ribbons
- 1 tablespoon olive oil
- 1 teaspoon garlic powder
- 1 teaspoon red pepper flakes
- 1 teaspoon salt
- 1 teaspoon freshly ground black pepper

1. Toss the cabbage with the olive oil, garlic powder, red pepper flakes, salt, and pepper in a large mixing bowl until well coated.
2. Transfer the cabbage to the baking pan.
3. Slide the baking pan into Rack Position 1, select Convection Bake, set temperature to 350ºF (180ºC), and set time to 7 minutes.
4. Flip the cabbage with tongs halfway through the cooking time.
5. When cooking is complete, the cabbage should be crisp. Remove from the oven to a plate and serve warm.

Cheesy Broccoli Gratin

Prep time: 5 minutes | Cook time: 14 minutes | Serves 2

- $1/_3$ cup fat-free milk
- 1 tablespoon all-purpose or gluten-free flour
- ½ tablespoon olive oil
- ½ teaspoon ground sage
- ¼ teaspoon kosher salt
- ⅛ teaspoon freshly ground black pepper
- 2 cups roughly chopped broccoli florets
- 6 tablespoons shredded Cheddar cheese
- 2 tablespoons panko bread crumbs
- 1 tablespoon grated Parmesan cheese
- Olive oil spray

1. Spritz the baking pan with olive oil spray.
2. Mix the milk, flour, olive oil, sage, salt, and pepper in a medium bowl and whisk to combine. Stir in the broccoli florets, Cheddar cheese, bread crumbs, and Parmesan cheese and toss to coat.
3. Pour the broccoli mixture into the prepared baking pan.
4. Slide the baking pan into Rack Position 1, select Convection Bake, set temperature to 330ºF (166ºC), and set time to 14 minutes.
5. When cooking is complete, the top should be golden brown and the broccoli should be tender. Remove from the oven and serve immediately.

Simple Zucchini Crisps

Prep time: 5 minutes | Cook time: 14 minutes | Serves 4

- 2 zucchinis, sliced into ¼- to ½-inch-thick rounds (about 2 cups)
- ¼ teaspoon garlic granules
- ⅛ teaspoon sea salt
- Freshly ground black pepper, to taste (optional)
- Cooking spray

1. Spritz the air fryer basket with cooking spray.
2. Put the zucchini rounds in the basket, spreading them out as much as possible. Top with a sprinkle of garlic granules, sea salt, and black pepper (if desired). Spritz the zucchini rounds with cooking spray.
3. Put the air fryer basket on the baking pan and slide into Rack Position 2, select Air Fry, set temperature to 392ºF (200ºC), and set time to 14 minutes.
4. Flip the zucchini rounds halfway through.
5. When cooking is complete, the zucchini rounds should be crisp-tender. Remove from the oven. Let them rest for 5 minutes and serve.

Crusted Brussels Sprouts with Sage

Prep time: 5 minutes | Cook time: 15 minutes | Serves 4

- 1 pound (454 g) Brussels sprouts, halved
- 1 cup bread crumbs
- 2 tablespoons grated Grana Padano
- cheese
- 1 tablespoon paprika
- 2 tablespoons canola oil
- 1 tablespoon chopped sage

1. Line the air fryer basket with parchment paper. Set aside.
2. In a small bowl, thoroughly mix the bread crumbs, cheese, and paprika. In a large bowl, place the Brussels sprouts and drizzle the canola oil over the top. Sprinkle with the bread crumb mixture and toss to coat.
3. Transfer the Brussels sprouts to the prepared basket.
4. Put the air fryer basket on the baking pan and slide into Rack Position 2, select Air Fry, set temperature to 400ºF (205ºC), and set time to 15 minutes.
5. Stir the Brussels a few times during cooking.
6. When cooking is complete, the Brussels sprouts should be lightly browned and crisp. Transfer the Brussels sprouts to a plate and sprinkle the sage on top before serving.

Rosemary Red Potatoes

Prep time: 5 minutes | Cook time: 20 minutes | Serves 4

- 1½ pounds (680 g) small red potatoes, cut into 1-inch cubes
- 2 tablespoons olive oil
- 2 tablespoons minced fresh rosemary
- 1 tablespoon minced garlic
- 1 teaspoon salt, plus additional as needed
- ½ teaspoon freshly ground black pepper, plus additional as needed

1. Toss the potato cubes with the olive oil, rosemary, garlic, salt, and pepper in a large bowl until thoroughly coated.
2. Arrange the potato cubes in the baking pan in a single layer.
3. Slide the baking pan into Rack Position 1, select Convection Bake, set temperature to 350ºF (180ºC), and set time to 20 minutes.
4. Stir the potatoes a few times during cooking for even cooking.
5. When cooking is complete, the potatoes should be tender. Remove from the oven to a plate. Taste and add additional salt and pepper as needed.

Chapter 3
Vegan and Vegetarian

Maple and Pecan Granola

Prep time: 5 minutes | Cook time: 20 minutes | Serves 4

- 1½ cups rolled oats
- ¼ cup maple syrup
- ¼ cup pecan pieces
- 1 teaspoon vanilla extract
- ½ teaspoon ground cinnamon

1. Line a baking sheet with parchment paper.
2. Mix together the oats, maple syrup, pecan pieces, vanilla, and cinnamon in a large bowl and stir until the oats and pecan pieces are completely coated. Spread the mixture evenly in the baking pan.
3. Slide the baking pan into Rack Position 1, select Convection Bake, set temperature to 300ºF (150ºC), and set time to 20 minutes.
4. Stir once halfway through the cooking time.
5. When done, remove from the oven and cool for 30 minutes before serving. The granola may still be a bit soft right after removing, but it will gradually firm up as it cools.

Rosemary Squash with Cheese

Prep time: 5 minutes | Cook time: 20 minutes | Serves 2

- 1 pound (454 g) butternut squash, cut into wedges
- 2 tablespoons olive oil
- 1 tablespoon dried rosemary
- Salt, to salt
- 1 cup crumbled goat cheese
- 1 tablespoon maple syrup

1. Toss the squash wedges with the olive oil, rosemary, and salt in a large bowl until well coated.
2. Transfer the squash wedges to the air fryer basket, spreading them out in as even a layer as possible.
3. Put the air fryer basket on the baking pan and slide into Rack Position 2, select Air Fry, set temperature to 350ºF (180ºC), and set time to 20 minutes.
4. After 10 minutes, remove from the oven and flip the squash. Return the pan to the oven and continue cooking for 10 minutes.
5. When cooking is complete, the squash should be golden brown. Remove from the oven. Sprinkle the goat cheese on top and serve drizzled with the maple syrup.

Spicy Thai-Style Vegetables

Prep time: 10 minutes | Cook time: 8 minutes | Serves 4

- 1 small head Napa cabbage, shredded, divided
- 1 medium carrot, cut into thin coins
- 8 ounces (227 g) snow peas
- 1 red or green bell pepper, sliced into thin strips
- 1 tablespoon vegetable oil
- 2 tablespoons soy sauce
- 1 tablespoon sesame oil
- 2 tablespoons brown sugar
- 2 tablespoons freshly squeezed lime juice
- 2 teaspoons red or green Thai curry paste
- 1 serrano chile, deseeded and minced
- 1 cup frozen mango slices, thawed
- ½ cup chopped roasted peanuts or cashews

1. Put half the Napa cabbage in a large bowl, along with the carrot, snow peas, and bell pepper. Drizzle with the vegetable oil and toss to coat. Spread them evenly in the air fryer basket.
2. Put the air fryer basket on the baking pan and slide into Rack Position 2, select Air Fry, set temperature to 375ºF (190ºC), and set time to 8 minutes.
3. Meanwhile, whisk together the soy sauce, sesame oil, brown sugar, lime juice, and curry paste in a small bowl.
4. When done, the vegetables should be tender and crisp. Remove from the oven and put the vegetables back into the bowl. Add the chile, mango slices, and the remaining cabbage. Pour over the dressing and toss to coat. Top with the roasted nuts and serve.

Cinnamon Celery Roots

Prep time: 10 minutes | Cook time: 20 minutes | Serves 4

- 2 celery roots, peeled and diced
- 1 teaspoon extra-virgin olive oil
- 1 teaspoon butter, melted
- ½ teaspoon ground cinnamon
- Sea salt and freshly ground black pepper, to taste

1. Line the baking pan with aluminum foil.
2. Toss the celery roots with the olive oil in a large bowl until well coated. Transfer them to the prepared baking pan.
3. Slide the baking pan into Rack Position 1, select Convection Bake, set temperature to 350ºF (180ºC), and set time to 20 minutes.
4. When done, the celery roots should be very tender. Remove from the oven to a serving bowl. Stir in the butter and cinnamon and mash them with a potato masher until fluffy.
5. Season with salt and pepper to taste. Serve immediately.

Paprika Cauliflower

Prep time: 10 minutes | Cook time: 20 minutes | Serves 4

- 1 large head cauliflower, broken into small florets
- 2 teaspoons smoked paprika
- 1 teaspoon garlic powder
- Salt and freshly ground black pepper, to taste
- Cooking spray

1. Spray the air fryer basket with cooking spray.
2. In a medium bowl, toss the cauliflower florets with the smoked paprika and garlic powder until evenly coated. Sprinkle with salt and pepper.
3. Place the cauliflower florets in the basket and lightly mist with cooking spray.
4. Put the air fryer basket on the baking pan and slide into Rack Position 2, select Air Fry, set temperature to 400ºF (205ºC), and set time to 20 minutes.
5. Stir the cauliflower four times during cooking.
6. Remove the cauliflower from the oven and serve hot.

Lemony Wax Beans

Prep time: 5 minutes | Cook time: 12 minutes | Serves 4

- 2 pounds (907 g) wax beans
- 2 tablespoons extra-virgin olive oil
- Salt and freshly ground black
- pepper, to taste
- Juice of ½ lemon, for serving

1. Line the air fryer basket with aluminum foil.
2. Toss the wax beans with the olive oil in a large bowl. Lightly season with salt and pepper.
3. Spread out the wax beans in the basket.
4. Put the air fryer basket on the baking pan and slide into Rack Position 2, select Air Fry, set temperature to 400ºF (205ºC), and set time to 12 minutes.
5. When done, the beans will be caramelized and tender. Remove from the oven to a plate and serve sprinkled with the lemon juice.

Easy Cheesy Vegetable Quesadilla

Prep time: 5 minutes | Cook time: 10 minutes | Serves 1

- 1 teaspoon olive oil
- 2 flour tortillas
- ¼ zucchini, sliced
- ¼ yellow bell pepper, sliced
- ¼ cup shredded gouda cheese
- 1 tablespoon chopped cilantro
- ½ green onion, sliced

1. Coat the air fryer basket with 1 teaspoon of olive oil.
2. Arrange a flour tortilla in the basket and scatter the top with zucchini, bell pepper, gouda cheese, cilantro, and green onion. Place the other flour tortilla on top.
3. Put the air fryer basket on the baking pan and slide into Rack Position 2, select Air Fry, set temperature to 390ºF (199ºC), and set time to 10 minutes.
4. When cooking is complete, the tortillas should be lightly browned and the vegetables should be tender. Remove from the oven and cool for 5 minutes before slicing into wedges.

Cheesy Cabbage Wedges

Prep time: 5 minutes | Cook time: 20 minutes | Serves 4

- 4 tablespoons melted butter
- 1 head cabbage, cut into wedges
- 1 cup shredded Parmesan cheese
- Salt and black pepper, to taste
- ½ cup shredded Mozzarella cheese

1. Brush the melted butter over the cut sides of cabbage wedges and sprinkle both sides with the Parmesan cheese. Season with salt and pepper to taste.
2. Place the cabbage wedges in the air fryer basket.
3. Put the air fryer basket on the baking pan and slide into Rack Position 2, select Air Fry, set temperature to 380ºF (193ºC), and set time to 20 minutes.
4. Flip the cabbage halfway through the cooking time.
5. When cooking is complete, the cabbage wedges should be lightly browned. Transfer the cabbage wedges to a plate and serve with the Mozzarella cheese sprinkled on top.

Mediterranean Baked Eggs with Spinach

Prep time: 10 minutes | Cook time: 10 minutes | Serves 2

- 2 tablespoons olive oil
- 4 eggs, whisked
- 5 ounces (142 g) fresh spinach, chopped
- 1 medium-sized tomato, chopped
- 1 teaspoon fresh lemon juice
- ½ teaspoon ground black pepper
- ½ teaspoon coarse salt
- ½ cup roughly chopped fresh basil leaves, for garnish

1. Generously grease the baking pan with olive oil.
2. Stir together the remaining ingredients except the basil leaves in the greased baking pan until well incorporated.
3. Slide the baking pan into Rack Position 1, select Convection Bake, set temperature to 280ºF (137ºC), and set time to 10 minutes.
4. When cooking is complete, the eggs should be completely set and the vegetables should be tender. Remove from the oven and serve garnished with the fresh basil leaves.

Herbed Broccoli with Cheese

Prep time: 5 minutes | Cook time: 18 minutes | Serves 4

- 1 large-sized head broccoli, stemmed and cut into small florets
- 2½ tablespoons canola oil
- 2 teaspoons dried basil
- 2 teaspoons dried rosemary
- Salt and ground black pepper, to taste
- $1/_3$ cup grated yellow cheese

1. Bring a pot of lightly salted water to a boil. Add the broccoli florets to the boiling water and let boil for about 3 minutes.
2. Drain the broccoli florets well and transfer to a large bowl. Add the canola oil, basil, rosemary, salt, and black pepper to the bowl and toss until the broccoli is fully coated. Place the broccoli in the air fryer basket.
3. Put the air fryer basket on the baking pan and slide into Rack Position 2, select Air Fry, set temperature to 390ºF (199ºC), and set time to 15 minutes.
4. Stir the broccoli halfway through the cooking time.
5. When cooking is complete, the broccoli should be crisp. Serve the broccoli warm with grated cheese sprinkled on top.

Asian-Inspired Broccoli

Prep time: 5 minutes | Cook time: 10 minutes | Serves 2

- 12 ounces (340 g) broccoli florets
- 2 tablespoons Asian hot chili oil
- 1 teaspoon ground Sichuan peppercorns (or black pepper)
- 2 garlic cloves, finely chopped
- 1 (2-inch) piece fresh ginger, peeled and finely chopped
- Kosher salt and freshly ground black pepper

1. Toss the broccoli florets with the chili oil, Sichuan peppercorns, garlic, ginger, salt, and pepper in a mixing bowl until thoroughly coated.
2. Transfer the broccoli florets to the air fryer basket.
3. Put the air fryer basket on the baking pan and slide into Rack Position 2, select Air Fry, set temperature to 375ºF (190ºC), and set time to 10 minutes.
4. Stir the broccoli florets halfway through the cooking time.
5. When cooking is complete, the broccoli florets should be lightly browned and tender. Remove the broccoli from the oven and serve on a plate.

Crispy Veggies with Halloumi

Prep time: 5 minutes | Cook time: 14 minutes | Serves 2

- 2 zucchinis, cut into even chunks
- 1 large eggplant, peeled, cut into chunks
- 1 large carrot, cut into chunks
- 6 ounces (170 g) halloumi cheese, cubed
- 2 teaspoons olive oil
- Salt and black pepper, to taste
- 1 teaspoon dried mixed herbs

1. Combine the zucchinis, eggplant, carrot, cheese, olive oil, salt, and pepper in a large bowl and toss to coat well.
2. Spread the mixture evenly in the air fryer basket.
3. Put the air fryer basket on the baking pan and slide into Rack Position 2, select Air Fry, set temperature to 340ºF (171ºC), and set time to 14 minutes.
4. Stir the mixture once during cooking.
5. When cooking is complete, they should be crispy and golden. Remove from the oven and serve topped with mixed herbs.

Air Fried Winter Vegetables

Prep time: 5 minutes | Cook time: 16 minutes | Serves 2

- 1 parsnip, sliced
- 1 cup sliced butternut squash
- 1 small red onion, cut into wedges
- ½ chopped celery stalk
- 1 tablespoon chopped fresh thyme
- 2 teaspoons olive oil
- Salt and black pepper, to taste

1. Toss all the ingredients in a large bowl until the vegetables are well coated.
2. Transfer the vegetables to the air fryer basket.
3. Put the air fryer basket on the baking pan and slide into Rack Position 2, select Air Fry, set temperature to 380ºF (193ºC), and set time to 16 minutes.
4. Stir the vegetables halfway through the cooking time.
5. When cooking is complete, the vegetables should be golden brown and tender. Remove from the oven and serve warm.

Crispy Tofu Sticks

Prep time: 5 minutes | Cook time: 14 minutes | Serves 4

- 2 tablespoons olive oil, divided
- ½ cup flour
- ½ cup crushed cornflakes
- Salt and black pepper, to taste
- 14 ounces (397 g) firm tofu, cut into ½-inch-thick strips

1. Grease the air fryer basket with 1 tablespoon of olive oil.
2. Combine the flour, cornflakes, salt, and pepper on a plate.
3. Dredge the tofu strips in the flour mixture until they are completely coated. Transfer the tofu strips to the greased basket.
4. Drizzle the remaining 1 tablespoon of olive oil over the top of tofu strips.
5. Put the air fryer basket on the baking pan and slide into Rack Position 2, select Air Fry, set temperature to 360ºF (182ºC), and set time to 14 minutes.
6. Flip the tofu strips halfway through the cooking time.
7. When cooking is complete, the tofu strips should be crispy. Remove from the oven and serve warm.

Balsamic Asparagus

Prep time: 15 minutes | Cook time: 10 minutes | Serves 4

- 4 tablespoons olive oil, plus more for greasing
- 4 tablespoons balsamic vinegar
- 1½ pounds (680 g) asparagus
- spears, trimmed
- Salt and freshly ground black pepper, to taste

1. Grease the air fryer basket with olive oil.
2. In a shallow bowl, stir together the 4 tablespoons of olive oil and balsamic vinegar to make a marinade.
3. Put the asparagus spears in the bowl so they are thoroughly covered by the marinade and allow to marinate for 5 minutes.
4. Put the asparagus in the greased basket in a single layer and season with salt and pepper.
5. Put the air fryer basket on the baking pan and slide into Rack Position 2, select Air Fry, set temperature to 350ºF (180ºC), and set time to 10 minutes.
6. Flip the asparagus halfway through the cooking time.
7. When done, the asparagus should be tender and lightly browned. Cool for 5 minutes before serving.

Chapter 4
Fish and Seafood

Crispy Fish Sticks

Prep time: 10 minutes | Cook time: 6 minutes | Serves 8

- 8 ounces (227 g) fish fillets (pollock or cod), cut into ½ × 3 inches strips
- Salt, to taste (optional)
- ½ cup plain bread crumbs
- Cooking spray

1. Season the fish strips with salt to taste, if desired.
2. Place the bread crumbs on a plate, then roll the fish in the bread crumbs until well coated. Spray all sides of the fish with cooking spray. Transfer to the air fryer basket in a single layer.
3. Put the air fryer basket on the baking pan and slide into Rack Position 2, select Air Fry, set temperature to 400ºF (205ºC), and set time to 6 minutes.
4. When cooked, the fish sticks should be golden brown and crispy. Remove from the oven to a plate and serve hot.

Tilapia Meunière with Vegetables

Prep time: 10 minutes | Cook time: 20 minutes | Serves 4

- 10 ounces (283 g) Yukon Gold potatoes, sliced ¼-inch thick
- 5 tablespoons unsalted butter, melted, divided
- 1 teaspoon kosher salt, divided
- 4 (8-ounce / 227-g) tilapia fillets
- ½ pound (227 g) green beans, trimmed
- Juice of 1 lemon
- 2 tablespoons chopped fresh parsley, for garnish

1. In a large bowl, drizzle the potatoes with 2 tablespoons of melted butter and ¼ teaspoon of kosher salt. Transfer the potatoes to the baking pan.
2. Slide the baking pan into Rack Position 1, select Convection Bake, set temperature to 375ºF (190ºC), and set time to 20 minutes.
3. Meanwhile, season both sides of the fillets with ½ teaspoon of kosher salt. Put the green beans in the medium bowl and sprinkle with the remaining ¼ teaspoon of kosher salt and 1 tablespoon of butter, tossing to coat.
4. After 10 minutes, remove from the oven and push the potatoes to one side. Put the fillets in the middle of the pan and add the green beans on the other side. Drizzle the remaining 2 tablespoons of butter over the fillets. Return the pan to the oven and continue cooking, or until the fish flakes easily with a fork and the green beans are crisp-tender.
5. When cooked, remove from the oven. Drizzle the lemon juice over the fillets and sprinkle the parsley on top for garnish. Serve hot.

Tuna Lettuce Wraps

Prep time: 10 minutes | Cook time: 4 to 7 minutes | Serves 4

- 1 pound (454 g) fresh tuna steak, cut into 1-inch cubes
- 2 garlic cloves, minced
- 1 tablespoon grated fresh ginger
- ½ teaspoon toasted sesame oil
- 4 low-sodium whole-wheat tortillas
- 2 cups shredded romaine lettuce
- 1 red bell pepper, thinly sliced
- ¼ cup low-fat mayonnaise

1. Combine the tuna cubes, garlic, ginger, and sesame oil in a medium bowl and toss until well coated. Allow to sit for 10 minutes.
2. When ready, place the tuna cubes in the air fryer basket.
3. Put the air fryer basket on the baking pan and slide into Rack Position 2, select Air Fry, set temperature to 390ºF (199ºC), and set time to 6 minutes.
4. When cooking is complete, the tuna cubes should be cooked through and golden brown. Remove the tuna cubes from the oven to a plate.
5. Make the wraps: Place the tortillas on a flat work surface and top each tortilla evenly with the cooked tuna, lettuce, bell pepper, and finish with the mayonnaise. Roll them up and serve immediately.

Teriyaki Salmon

Prep time: 15 minutes | Cook time: 15 minutes | Serves 4

- ¾ cup Teriyaki sauce, divided
- 4 (6-ounce / 170-g) skinless salmon fillets
- 4 heads baby bok choy, root ends trimmed off and cut in half
- lengthwise through the root
- 1 teaspoon sesame oil
- 1 tablespoon vegetable oil
- 1 tablespoon toasted sesame seeds

1. Set aside ¼ cup of Teriyaki sauce and pour the remaining sauce into a resealable plastic bag. Put the salmon into the bag and seal, squeezing as much air out as possible. Allow the salmon to marinate for at least 10 minutes.
2. Arrange the bok choy halves in the baking pan. Drizzle the oils over the vegetables, tossing to coat. Drizzle about 1 tablespoon of the reserved Teriyaki sauce over the bok choy, then push them to the sides of the pan.
3. Put the salmon fillets in the middle of the pan.
4. Slide the baking pan into Rack Position 1, select Convection Bake, set temperature to 375ºF (190ºC), and set time to 15 minutes.
5. When done, remove the pan and brush the salmon with the remaining Teriyaki sauce. Serve garnished with the sesame seeds.

Herbed Salmon with Asparagus

Prep time: 5 minutes | Cook time: 12 minutes | Serves 2

- 2 teaspoons olive oil, plus additional for drizzling
- 2 (5-ounce / 142-g) salmon fillets, with skin
- Salt and freshly ground black pepper, to taste
- 1 bunch asparagus, trimmed
- 1 teaspoon dried tarragon
- 1 teaspoon dried chives
- Fresh lemon wedges, for serving

1. Rub the olive oil all over the salmon fillets. Sprinkle with salt and pepper to taste.
2. Put the asparagus on the foil-lined baking pan and place the salmon fillets on top, skin-side down.
3. Slide the baking pan into Rack Position 1, select Convection Bake, set temperature to 350ºF (180ºC), and set time to 12 minutes.
4. When cooked, the fillets should register 145ºF (63ºC) on an instant-read thermometer. Remove from the oven and cut the salmon fillets in half crosswise, then use a metal spatula to lift flesh from skin and transfer to a serving plate. Discard the skin and drizzle the salmon fillets with additional olive oil. Scatter with the herbs.
5. Serve the salmon fillets with asparagus spears and lemon wedges on the side.

Homemade Fish Sticks

Prep time: 10 minutes | Cook time: 8 minutes | Makes 8 fish sticks

- 8 ounces (227 g) fish fillets (pollock or cod), cut into ½×3-inch strips
- Salt, to taste (optional)
- ½ cup plain bread crumbs
- Cooking spray

1. Season the fish strips with salt to taste, if desired.
2. Place the bread crumbs on a plate. Roll the fish strips in the bread crumbs to coat. Spritz the fish strips with cooking spray.
3. Arrange the fish strips in the air fryer basket in a single layer.
4. Put the air fryer basket on the baking pan and slide into Rack Position 2, select Air Fry, set temperature to 390ºF (199ºC), and set time to 8 minutes.
5. When cooking is complete, they should be golden brown. Remove from the oven and cool for 5 minutes before serving.

Easy Salmon Patties

Prep time: 5 minutes | Cook time: 11 minutes | Makes 6 patties

- 1 (14.75-ounce / 418-g) can Alaskan pink salmon, drained and bones removed
- ½ cup bread crumbs
- 1 egg, whisked
- 2 scallions, diced
- 1 teaspoon garlic powder
- Salt and pepper, to taste
- Cooking spray

1. Stir together the salmon, bread crumbs, whisked egg, scallions, garlic powder, salt, and pepper in a large bowl until well incorporated.
2. Divide the salmon mixture into six equal portions and form each into a patty with your hands.
3. Arrange the salmon patties in the air fryer basket and spritz them with cooking spray.
4. Put the air fryer basket on the baking pan and slide into Rack Position 2, select Air Fry, set temperature to 400ºF (205ºC), and set time to 10 minutes.
5. Flip the patties once halfway through.
6. When cooking is complete, the patties should be golden brown and cooked through. Remove the patties from the oven and serve on a plate.

Basil Salmon with Tomatoes

Prep time: 10 minutes | Cook time: 15 minutes | Serves 4

- 4 (6-ounce / 170-g) salmon fillets, patted dry
- 1 teaspoon kosher salt, divided
- 2 pints cherry or grape tomatoes, halved if large, divided
- 3 tablespoons extra-virgin olive oil, divided
- 2 garlic cloves, minced
- 1 small red bell pepper, deseeded and chopped
- 2 tablespoons chopped fresh basil, divided

1. Season both sides of the salmon with ½ teaspoon of kosher salt.
2. Put about half of the tomatoes in a large bowl, along with the remaining ½ teaspoon of kosher salt, 2 tablespoons of olive oil, garlic, bell pepper, and 1 tablespoon of basil. Toss to coat and then transfer to the baking pan.
3. Arrange the salmon fillets in the pan, skin-side down. Brush them with the remaining 1 tablespoon of olive oil.
4. Slide the baking pan into Rack Position 1, select Convection Bake, set temperature to 375ºF (190ºC), and set time to 15 minutes.
5. After 7 minutes, remove the pan and fold in the remaining tomatoes. Return the pan to the oven and continue cooking.
6. When cooked, remove from the oven. Serve sprinkled with the remaining 1 tablespoon of basil.

Cajun and Lemon Pepper Cod

Prep time: 5 minutes | Cook time: 12 minutes | Makes 2 cod fillets

- 1 tablespoon Cajun seasoning
- 1 teaspoon salt
- ½ teaspoon lemon pepper
- ½ teaspoon freshly ground black pepper
- 2 (8-ounce / 227-g) cod fillets, cut

- to fit into the air fryer basket
- Cooking spray
- 2 tablespoons unsalted butter, melted
- 1 lemon, cut into 4 wedges

1. Spritz the baking pan with cooking spray.
2. Thoroughly combine the Cajun seasoning, salt, lemon pepper, and black pepper in a small bowl. Rub this mixture all over the cod fillets until completely coated.
3. Put the fillets in the prepared pan and brush the melted butter over both sides of each fillet.
4. Slide the baking pan into Rack Position 1, select Convection Bake, set temperature to 360ºF (182ºC), and set time to 12 minutes.
5. Flip the fillets halfway through the cooking time.
6. When cooking is complete, the fish should flake apart with a fork. Remove the fillets from the oven and serve with fresh lemon wedges.

Baked Halibut Steaks with Parsley

Prep time: 5 minutes | Cook time: 10 minutes | Serves 4

- 1 pound (454 g) halibut steaks
- ¼ cup vegetable oil
- 2½ tablespoons Worcester sauce
- 2 tablespoons honey
- 2 tablespoons vermouth
- 1 tablespoon freshly squeezed

- lemon juice
- 1 tablespoon fresh parsley leaves, coarsely chopped
- Salt and pepper, to taste
- 1 teaspoon dried basil

1. Put all the ingredients in a large mixing dish and gently stir until the fish is coated evenly. Transfer the fish to the baking pan.
2. Slide the baking pan into Rack Position 1, select Convection Bake, set temperature to 375ºF (190ºC), and set time to 10 minutes.
3. Flip the fish halfway through cooking time.
4. When cooking is complete, the fish should reach an internal temperature of at least 145ºF (63ºC) on a meat thermometer. Remove from the oven and let the fish cool for 5 minutes before serving.

Paprika Shrimp

Prep time: 5 minutes | Cook time: 10 minutes | Serves 4

- 1 pound (454 g) tiger shrimp
- 2 tablespoons olive oil
- ½ tablespoon old bay seasoning
- ¼ tablespoon smoked paprika
- ¼ teaspoon cayenne pepper
- A pinch of sea salt

1. Toss all the ingredients in a large bowl until the shrimp are evenly coated.
2. Arrange the shrimp in the air fryer basket.
3. Put the air fryer basket on the baking pan and slide into Rack Position 2, select Air Fry, set temperature to 380ºF (193ºC), and set time to 10 minutes.
4. When cooking is complete, the shrimp should be pink and cooked through. Remove from the oven and serve hot.

Breaded Fish Fillets

Prep time: 20 minutes | Cook time: 7 minutes | Serves 4

- 1 pound (454 g) fish fillets
- 1 tablespoon coarse brown mustard
- 1 teaspoon Worcestershire sauce
- ½ teaspoon hot sauce
- Salt, to taste
- Cooking spray
- Crumb Coating:
- ¾ cup panko bread crumbs
- ¼ cup stone-ground cornmeal
- ¼ teaspoon salt

1. On your cutting board, cut the fish fillets crosswise into slices, about 1 inch wide.
2. In a small bowl, stir together the mustard, Worcestershire sauce, and hot sauce to make a paste and rub this paste on all sides of the fillets. Season with salt to taste.
3. In a shallow bowl, thoroughly combine all the ingredients for the crumb coating and spread them on a sheet of wax paper.
4. Roll the fish fillets in the crumb mixture until thickly coated. Spritz all sides of the fish with cooking spray, then arrange them in the air fryer basket in a single layer.
5. Put the air fryer basket on the baking pan and slide into Rack Position 2, select Air Fry, set temperature to 400ºF (205ºC), and set time to 7 minutes.
6. When cooking is complete, the fish should flake apart with a fork. Remove from the oven and serve warm.

Golden Beer-Battered Cod

Prep time: 5 minutes | Cook time: 15 minutes | Serves 4

- 2 eggs
- 1 cup malty beer
- 1 cup all-purpose flour
- ½ cup cornstarch
- 1 teaspoon garlic powder
- Salt and pepper, to taste
- 4 (4-ounce / 113-g) cod fillets
- Cooking spray

1. In a shallow bowl, beat together the eggs with the beer. In another shallow bowl, thoroughly combine the flour and cornstarch. Sprinkle with the garlic powder, salt, and pepper.
2. Dredge each cod fillet in the flour mixture, then in the egg mixture. Dip each piece of fish in the flour mixture a second time.
3. Spritz the air fryer basket with cooking spray. Arrange the cod fillets in the pan in a single layer.
4. Put the air fryer basket on the baking pan and slide into Rack Position 2, select Air Fry, set temperature to 400ºF (205ºC), and set time to 15 minutes.
5. Flip the fillets halfway through the cooking time.
6. When cooking is complete, the cod should reach an internal temperature of 145ºF (63ºC) on a meat thermometer and the outside should be crispy. Let the fish cool for 5 minutes and serve.

Easy Shrimp and Vegetable Paella

Prep time: 5 minutes | Cook time: 16 minutes | Serves 4

- 1 (10-ounce / 284-g) package frozen cooked rice, thawed
- 1 (6-ounce / 170-g) jar artichoke hearts, drained and chopped
- ¼ cup vegetable broth
- ½ teaspoon dried thyme
- ½ teaspoon turmeric
- 1 cup frozen cooked small shrimp
- ½ cup frozen baby peas
- 1 tomato, diced

1. Mix together the cooked rice, chopped artichoke hearts, vegetable broth, thyme, and turmeric in the baking pan and stir to combine.
2. Slide the baking pan into Rack Position 1, select Convection Bake, set temperature to 340ºF (171ºC), and set time to 16 minutes.
3. After 9 minutes, remove from the oven and add the shrimp, baby peas, and diced tomato to the baking pan. Mix well. Return the pan to the oven and continue cooking for 7 minutes more, or until the shrimp are done and the paella is bubbling.
4. When cooking is complete, remove from the oven. Cool for 5 minutes before serving.

Garlicky Cod Fillets

Prep time: 10 minutes | Cook time: 12 minutes | Serves 4

- 1 teaspoon olive oil
- 4 cod fillets
- ¼ teaspoon fine sea salt
- ¼ teaspoon ground black pepper, or more to taste
- 1 teaspoon cayenne pepper
- ½ cup fresh Italian parsley, coarsely chopped
- ½ cup nondairy milk
- 1 Italian pepper, chopped
- 4 garlic cloves, minced
- 1 teaspoon dried basil
- ½ teaspoon dried oregano

1. Lightly coat the sides and bottom of the baking pan with the olive oil. Set aside.
2. In a large bowl, sprinkle the fillets with salt, black pepper, and cayenne pepper.
3. In a food processor, pulse the remaining ingredients until smoothly puréed.
4. Add the purée to the bowl of fillets and toss to coat, then transfer to the prepared baking pan.
5. Slide the baking pan into Rack Position 1, select Convection Bake, set temperature to 380ºF (193ºC), and set time to 12 minutes.
6. When cooking is complete, the fish should flake when pressed lightly with a fork. Remove from the oven and serve warm.

Spiced Red Snapper

Prep time: 13 minutes | Cook time: 10 minutes | Serves 4

- 1 teaspoon olive oil
- 1½ teaspoons black pepper
- ¼ teaspoon garlic powder
- ¼ teaspoon thyme
- ⅛ teaspoon cayenne pepper
- 4 (4-ounce / 113-g) red snapper fillets, skin on
- 4 thin slices lemon
- Nonstick cooking spray

1. Spritz the baking pan with nonstick cooking spray.
2. In a small bowl, stir together the olive oil, black pepper, garlic powder, thyme, and cayenne pepper. Rub the mixture all over the fillets until completely coated.
3. Lay the fillets, skin-side down, in the baking pan and top each fillet with a slice of lemon.
4. Slide the baking pan into Rack Position 1, select Convection Bake, set temperature to 390ºF (199ºC), and set time to 10 minutes.
5. Flip the fillets halfway through the cooking time.
6. When cooking is complete, the fish should be cooked through. Let the fish cool for 5 minutes and serve.

Parmesan-Crusted Halibut Fillets

Prep time: 5 minutes | Cook time: 10 minutes | Serves 4

- 2 medium-sized halibut fillets
- Dash of tabasco sauce
- 1 teaspoon curry powder
- ½ teaspoon ground coriander
- ½ teaspoon hot paprika
- Kosher salt and freshly cracked mixed peppercorns, to taste
- 2 eggs
- 1½ tablespoons olive oil
- ½ cup grated Parmesan cheese

1. On a clean work surface, drizzle the halibut fillets with the tabasco sauce. Sprinkle with the curry powder, coriander, hot paprika, salt, and cracked mixed peppercorns. Set aside.
2. In a shallow bowl, beat the eggs until frothy. In another shallow bowl, combine the olive oil and Parmesan cheese.
3. One at a time, dredge the halibut fillets in the beaten eggs, shaking off any excess, then roll them over the Parmesan cheese until evenly coated.
4. Arrange the halibut fillets in the baking pan in a single layer.
5. Slide the baking pan into Rack Position 1, select Convection Bake, set temperature to 365ºF (185ºC), and set time to 10 minutes.
6. When cooking is complete, the fish should be golden brown and crisp. Cool for 5 minutes before serving.

Pecan-Crusted Catfish Fillets

Prep time: 5 minutes | Cook time: 12 minutes | Serves 4

- ½ cup pecan meal
- 1 teaspoon fine sea salt
- ¼ teaspoon ground black pepper
- 4 (4-ounce / 113-g) catfish fillets
- Avocado oil spray
- For Garnish (Optional):
- Fresh oregano
- Pecan halves

1. Spray the air fryer basket with avocado oil spray.
2. Combine the pecan meal, sea salt, and black pepper in a large bowl. Dredge each catfish fillet in the meal mixture, turning until well coated. Spritz the fillets with avocado oil spray, then transfer to the basket.
3. Put the air fryer basket on the baking pan and slide into Rack Position 2, select Air Fry, set temperature to 375ºF (190ºC), and set time to 12 minutes.
4. Flip the fillets halfway through the cooking time.
5. When cooking is complete, the fish should be cooked through and no longer translucent. Remove from the oven and sprinkle the oregano sprigs and pecan halves on top for garnish, if desired. Serve immediately.

Coconut Chili Fish Curry

Prep time: 10 minutes | Cook time: 22 minutes | Serves 4

- 2 tablespoons sunflower oil, divided
- 1 pound (454 g) fish, chopped
- 1 ripe tomato, pureéd
- 2 red chilies, chopped
- 1 shallot, minced
- 1 garlic clove, minced
- 1 cup coconut milk
- 1 tablespoon coriander powder
- 1 teaspoon red curry paste
- ½ teaspoon fenugreek seeds
- Salt and white pepper, to taste

1. Coat the air fryer basket with 1 tablespoon of sunflower oil. Place the fish in the basket.
2. Put the air fryer basket on the baking pan and slide into Rack Position 2, select Air Fry, set temperature to 380ºF (193ºC), and set time to 10 minutes.
3. Flip the fish halfway through the cooking time.
4. When cooking is complete, transfer the cooked fish to the baking pan greased with the remaining 1 tablespoon of sunflower oil. Stir in the remaining ingredients.
5. Put the air fryer basket on the baking pan and slide into Rack Position 2, select Air Fry, set temperature to 350ºF (180ºC), and set time to 12 minutes.
6. When cooking is complete, they should be heated through. Cool for 5 to 8 minutes before serving.

Spicy Orange Shrimp

Prep time: 40 minutes | Cook time: 12 minutes | Serves 4

- ⅓ cup orange juice
- 3 teaspoons minced garlic
- 1 teaspoon Old Bay seasoning
- ¼ to ½ teaspoon cayenne pepper
- 1 pound (454 g) medium shrimp, thawed, deveined, peeled, with tails off, and patted dry
- Cooking spray

1. Stir together the orange juice, garlic, Old Bay seasoning, and cayenne pepper in a medium bowl. Add the shrimp to the bowl and toss to coat well.
2. Cover the bowl with plastic wrap and marinate in the refrigerator for 30 minutes.
3. Spritz the air fryer basket with cooking spray. Place the shrimp in the pan and spray with cooking spray.
4. Put the air fryer basket on the baking pan and slide into Rack Position 2, select Air Fry, set temperature to 400ºF (205ºC), and set time to 12 minutes.
5. Flip the shrimp halfway through the cooking time.
6. When cooked, the shrimp should be opaque and crisp. Remove from the oven and serve hot.

Browned Shrimp Patties

Prep time: 15 minutes | Cook time: 12 minutes | Serves 4

- ½ pound (227 g) raw shrimp, shelled, deveined, and chopped finely
- 2 cups cooked sushi rice
- ¼ cup chopped red bell pepper
- ¼ cup chopped celery
- ¼ cup chopped green onion
- 2 teaspoons Worcestershire sauce
- ½ teaspoon salt
- ½ teaspoon garlic powder
- ½ teaspoon Old Bay seasoning
- ½ cup plain bread crumbs
- Cooking spray

1. Put all the ingredients except the bread crumbs and oil in a large bowl and stir to incorporate.
2. Scoop out the shrimp mixture and shape into 8 equal-sized patties with your hands, no more than ½-inch thick. Roll the patties in the bread crumbs on a plate and spray both sides with cooking spray. Place the patties in the air fryer basket.
3. Put the air fryer basket on the baking pan and slide into Rack Position 2, select Air Fry, set temperature to 390ºF (199ºC), and set time to 12 minutes.
4. Flip the patties halfway through the cooking time.
5. When cooking is complete, the outside should be crispy brown. Divide the patties among four plates and serve warm.

Chapter 5 Poultry

Cheese-Encrusted Chicken Tenderloins with Peanuts

Prep time: 10 minutes | Cook time: 12 minutes | Serves 4

- ½ cup grated Parmesan cheese
- ½ teaspoon garlic powder
- 1 teaspoon red pepper flakes
- Sea salt and ground black pepper, to taste
- 2 tablespoons peanut oil
- 1½ pounds (680 g) chicken tenderloins
- 2 tablespoons peanuts, roasted and roughly chopped
- Cooking spray

1. Spritz the air fryer basket with cooking spray.
2. Combine the Parmesan cheese, garlic powder, red pepper flakes, salt, black pepper, and peanut oil in a large bow. Stir to mix well.
3. Dip the chicken tenderloins in the cheese mixture, then press to coat well. Shake the excess off.
4. Transfer the chicken tenderloins in the basket.
5. Put the air fryer basket on the baking pan and slide into Rack Position 2, select Air Fry, set temperature to 360ºF (182ºC) and set time to 12 minutes.
6. Flip the tenderloin halfway through.
7. When cooking is complete, the tenderloin should be well browned.
8. Transfer the chicken tenderloins on a large plate and top with roasted peanuts before serving.

Simple Herbed Hens

Prep time: 2 hours 15 minutes | Cook time: 30 minutes | Serves 8

- 4 (1¼-pound / 567-g) Cornish hens, giblets removed, split lengthwise
- 2 cups white wine, divided
- 2 garlic cloves, minced
- 1 small onion, minced
- ½ teaspoon celery seeds
- ½ teaspoon poultry seasoning
- ½ teaspoon paprika
- ½ teaspoon dried oregano
- ¼ teaspoon freshly ground black pepper

1. Place the hens, cavity side up, in the baking pan. Pour 1½ cups of the wine over the hens. Set aside.
2. In a shallow bowl, combine the garlic, onion, celery seeds, poultry seasoning, paprika, oregano, and pepper. Sprinkle half of the combined seasonings over the cavity of each split half. Cover and refrigerate. Allow the hens to marinate for 2 hours.
3. Transfer the hens to the pan. Slide the baking pan into Rack Position 1, select Convection Bake, set temperature to 350ºF (180ºC) and set time to 90 minutes.
4. Flip the breast halfway through and remove the skin. Pour the remaining ½ cup of wine over the top, and sprinkle with the remaining seasonings.
5. When cooking is complete, the inner temperature of the hens should be at least 165ºF (74ºC). Transfer the hens to a serving platter and serve hot.

Pineapple Chicken

Prep time: 10 minutes | Cook time: 10 minutes | Serves 6

- 1½ pounds (680 g) boneless, skinless chicken breasts, cut into 1-inch chunks
- ¾ cup soy sauce
- 2 tablespoons ketchup
- 2 tablespoons brown sugar
- 2 tablespoons rice vinegar
- 1 red bell pepper, cut into 1-inch chunks
- 1 green bell pepper, cut into 1-inch chunks
- 6 scallions, cut into 1-inch pieces
- 1 cup (¾-inch chunks) fresh pineapple, rinsed and drained
- Cooking spray

1. Place the chicken in a large bowl. Add the soy sauce, ketchup, brown sugar, vinegar, red and green peppers, and scallions. Toss to coat.
2. Spritz the baking pan with cooking spray and place the chicken and vegetables in the pan.
3. Slide the baking pan into Rack Position 1, select Convection Bake, set temperature to 375ºF (190ºC), and set time to 10 minutes.
4. After 6 minutes, remove from the oven. Add the pineapple chunks to the pan and stir. Return the pan to the oven and continue cooking.
5. When cooking is complete, remove from the oven. Serve with steamed rice, if desired.

Bell Pepper Stuffed Chicken Roll-Ups

Prep time: 10 minutes | Cook time: 12 minutes | Serves 4

- 2 (4-ounce / 113-g) boneless, skinless chicken breasts, slice in half horizontally
- 1 tablespoon olive oil
- Juice of ½ lime
- 2 tablespoons taco seasoning
- ½ green bell pepper, cut into strips
- ½ red bell pepper, cut into strips
- ¼ onion, sliced

1. Unfold the chicken breast slices on a clean work surface. Rub with olive oil, then drizzle with lime juice and sprinkle with taco seasoning.
2. Top the chicken slices with equal amount of bell peppers and onion. Roll them up and secure with toothpicks.
3. Arrange the chicken roll-ups in the basket.
4. Put the air fryer basket on the baking pan and slide into Rack Position 2, select Air Fry, set temperature to 400ºF (205ºC) and set time to 12 minutes.
5. Flip the chicken roll-ups halfway through.
6. When cooking is complete, the internal temperature of the chicken should reach at least 165ºF (74ºC).
7. Remove the chicken from the oven. Discard the toothpicks and serve immediately.

Honey Glazed Chicken Breasts

Prep time: 5 minutes | Cook time: 10 minutes | Serves 4

- 4 (4-ounce / 113-g) boneless, skinless chicken breasts
- Chicken seasoning or rub, to taste
- Salt and ground black pepper, to taste
- ¼ cup honey
- 2 tablespoons soy sauce
- 2 teaspoons grated fresh ginger
- 2 garlic cloves, minced
- Cooking spray

1. Spritz the air fryer basket with cooking spray.
2. Rub the chicken breasts with chicken seasoning, salt, and black pepper on a clean work surface.
3. Arrange the chicken breasts in the basket and spritz with cooking spray.
4. Put the air fryer basket on the baking pan and slide into Rack Position 2, select Air Fry, set temperature to 400ºF (205ºC) and set time to 10 minutes.
5. Flip the chicken breasts halfway through.
6. When cooking is complete, the internal temperature of the thickest part of the chicken should reach at least 165ºF (74ºC).
7. Meanwhile, combine the honey, soy sauce, ginger, and garlic in a saucepan and heat over medium-high heat for 3 minutes or until thickened. Stir constantly.
8. Remove the chicken from the oven and serve with the honey glaze.

Lime Chicken with Cilantro

Prep time: 35 minutes | Cook time: 10 minutes | Serves 4

- 4 (4-ounce / 113-g) boneless, skinless chicken breasts
- ½ cup chopped fresh cilantro
- Juice of 1 lime
- Chicken seasoning or rub, to taste
- Salt and ground black pepper, to taste
- Cooking spray

1. Put the chicken breasts in the large bowl, then add the cilantro, lime juice, chicken seasoning, salt, and black pepper. Toss to coat well.
2. Wrap the bowl in plastic and refrigerate to marinate for at least 30 minutes.
3. Spritz the air fryer basket with cooking spray.
4. Remove the marinated chicken breasts from the bowl and place in the basket. Spritz with cooking spray.
5. Put the air fryer basket on the baking pan and slide into Rack Position 2, select Air Fry, set temperature to 400ºF (205ºC) and set time to 10 minutes.
6. Flip the breasts halfway through.
7. When cooking is complete, the internal temperature of the chicken should reach at least 165ºF (74ºC).
8. Serve immediately.

Simple Whole Chicken Bake

Prep time: 10 minutes | Cook time: 1 hour | Serves 2 to 4

- ½ cup melted butter
- 3 tablespoons garlic, minced
- Salt, to taste
- 1 teaspoon ground black pepper
- 1 (1-pound / 454-g) whole chicken

1. Combine the butter with garlic, salt, and ground black pepper in a small bowl.
2. Brush the butter mixture over the whole chicken, then place the chicken in the baking pan, skin side down.
3. Slide the baking pan into Rack Position 1, select Convection Bake, set temperature to 350ºF (180ºC) and set time to 60 minutes.
4. Flip the chicken halfway through.
5. When cooking is complete, an instant-read thermometer inserted in the thickest part of the chicken should register at least 165ºF (74ºC).
6. Remove the chicken from the oven and allow to cool for 15 minutes before serving.

Peach and Cherry Chicken

Prep time: 8 minutes | Cook time: 15 minutes | Serves 4

- $1/_3$ cup peach preserves
- 1 teaspoon ground rosemary
- ½ teaspoon black pepper
- ½ teaspoon salt
- ½ teaspoon marjoram
- 1 teaspoon light olive oil
- 1 pound (454 g) boneless chicken breasts, cut in 1½-inch chunks
- 1 (10-ounce / 284-g) package frozen dark cherries, thawed and drained
- Cooking spray

1. In a medium bowl, mix peach preserves, rosemary, pepper, salt, marjoram, and olive oil.
2. Stir in chicken chunks and toss to coat well with the preserve mixture.
3. Spritz the baking pan with cooking spray and lay chicken chunks in the pan.
4. Slide the baking pan into Rack Position 1, select Convection Bake, set the temperature to 400ºF (205ºC) and set the time to 15 minutes.
5. After 7 minutes, remove from the oven and flip the chicken chunks. Return the pan to the oven and continue cooking.
6. When cooking is complete, the chicken should no longer pink and the juices should run clear.
7. Scatter the cherries over and cook for an additional minute to heat cherries.
8. Serve immediately.

Golden Chicken Cutlets

Prep time: 15 minutes | Cook time: 15 minutes | Serves 4

- 2 tablespoons panko bread crumbs
- ¼ cup grated Parmesan cheese
- ⅛ tablespoon paprika
- ½ tablespoon garlic powder
- 2 large eggs
- 4 chicken cutlets
- 1 tablespoon parsley
- Salt and ground black pepper, to taste
- Cooking spray

1. Spritz the air fryer basket with cooking spray.
2. Combine the bread crumbs, Parmesan, paprika, garlic powder, salt, and ground black pepper in a large bowl. Stir to mix well. Beat the eggs in a separate bowl.
3. Dredge the chicken cutlets in the beaten eggs, then roll over the bread crumbs mixture to coat well. Shake the excess off.
4. Transfer the chicken cutlets in the basket and spritz with cooking spray.
5. Put the air fryer basket on the baking pan and slide into Rack Position 2, select Air Fry, set temperature to 400ºF (205ºC) and set time to 15 minutes.
6. Flip the cutlets halfway through.
7. When cooking is complete, the cutlets should be crispy and golden brown.
8. Serve with parsley on top.

Deep Fried Duck Leg Quarters

Prep time: 5 minutes | Cook time: 45 minutes | Serves 4

- 4 (½-pound / 227-g) skin-on duck leg quarters
- 2 medium garlic cloves, minced
- ½ teaspoon salt
- ½ teaspoon ground black pepper

1. Spritz the air fryer basket with cooking spray.
2. On a clean work surface, rub the duck leg quarters with garlic, salt, and black pepper.
3. Arrange the leg quarters in the basket and spritz with cooking spray.
4. Put the air fryer basket on the baking pan and slide into Rack Position 2, select Air Fry, set temperature to 300ºF (150ºC) and set time to 30 minutes.
5. After 30 minutes, remove from the oven. Flip the leg quarters. Increase temperature to 375ºF (190ºC) and set time to 15 minutes. Return to the oven and continue cooking.
6. When cooking is complete, the leg quarters should be well browned and crispy.
7. Remove the duck leg quarters from the oven and allow to cool for 10 minutes before serving.

China Spicy Turkey Thighs

Prep time: 10 minutes | Cook time: 25 minutes | Serves 6

- 2 pounds (907 g) turkey thighs
- 1 teaspoon Chinese five-spice powder
- ¼ teaspoon Sichuan pepper
- 1 teaspoon pink Himalayan salt
- 1 tablespoon Chinese rice vinegar
- 1 tablespoon mustard
- 1 tablespoon chili sauce
- 2 tablespoons soy sauce
- Cooking spray

1. Spritz the air fryer basket with cooking spray.
2. Rub the turkey thighs with five-spice powder, Sichuan pepper, and salt on a clean work surface.
3. Put the turkey thighs in the basket and spritz with cooking spray.
4. Put the air fryer basket on the baking pan and slide into Rack Position 2, select Air Fry, set temperature to 360ºF (182ºC) and set time to 22 minutes.
5. Flip the thighs at least three times during the cooking.
6. When cooking is complete, the thighs should be well browned.
7. Meanwhile, heat the remaining ingredients in a saucepan over medium-high heat. Cook for 3 minutes or until the sauce is thickened and reduces to two thirds.
8. Transfer the thighs onto a plate and baste with sauce before serving.

Creole Hens

Prep time: 10 minutes | Cook time: 40 minutes | Serves 4

- ½ tablespoon Creole seasoning
- ½ tablespoon garlic powder
- ½ tablespoon onion powder
- ½ tablespoon freshly ground black pepper
- ½ tablespoon paprika
- 2 tablespoons olive oil
- 2 Cornish hens
- Cooking spray

1. Spritz the air fryer basket with cooking spray.
2. In a small bowl, mix the Creole seasoning, garlic powder, onion powder, pepper, and paprika.
3. Pat the Cornish hens dry and brush each hen all over with the olive oil. Rub each hen with the seasoning mixture. Place the Cornish hens in the basket.
4. Put the air fryer basket on the baking pan and slide into Rack Position 2, select Air Fry, set the temperature to 375ºF (190ºC) and set the time to 30 minutes.
5. After 15 minutes, remove from the oven. Flip the hens over and baste it with any drippings collected in the bottom drawer of the oven. Return to the oven and continue cooking.
6. When cooking is complete, a thermometer inserted into the thickest part of the hens should reach at least 165ºF (74ºC).
7. Let the hens rest for 10 minutes before carving.

Balsamic Chicken Breast Roast

Prep time: 35 minutes | Cook time: 40 minutes | Serves 2

- ¼ cup balsamic vinegar
- 2 teaspoons dried oregano
- 2 garlic cloves, minced
- 1 tablespoon olive oil
- ⅛ teaspoon salt
- ½ teaspoon freshly ground black pepper
- 2 (4-ounce / 113-g) boneless, skinless, chicken-breast halves
- Cooking spray

1. In a small bowl, add the vinegar, oregano, garlic, olive oil, salt, and pepper. Mix to combine.
2. Put the chicken in a resealable plastic bag. Pour the vinegar mixture in the bag with the chicken, seal the bag, and shake to coat the chicken. Refrigerate for 30 minutes to marinate.
3. Spritz the baking pan with cooking spray. Put the chicken in the prepared baking pan and pour the marinade over the chicken.
4. Slide the baking pan into Rack Position 1, select Convection Bake, set temperature to 400ºF (205ºC) and set time to 40 minutes.
5. After 20 minutes, remove the pan from the oven. Flip the chicken. Return the pan to the oven and continue cooking.
6. When cooking is complete, the internal temperature of the chicken should registers at least 165ºF (74ºC).
7. Let sit for 5 minutes, then serve.

Duck Breasts with Marmalade Balsamic Glaze

Prep time: 5 minutes | Cook time: 13 minutes | Serves 4

- 4 (6-ounce / 170-g) skin-on duck breasts
- 1 teaspoon salt
- ¼ cup orange marmalade
- 1 tablespoon white balsamic vinegar
- ¾ teaspoon ground black pepper

1. Cut 10 slits into the skin of the duck breasts, then sprinkle with salt on both sides.
2. Place the breasts in the air fryer basket, skin side up.
3. Put the air fryer basket on the baking pan and slide into Rack Position 2, select Air Fry, set temperature to 400ºF (205ºC) and set time to 10 minutes.
4. Meanwhile, combine the remaining ingredients in a small bowl. Stir to mix well.
5. When cooking is complete, brush the duck skin with the marmalade mixture. Flip the breast and air fry for 3 more minutes or until the skin is crispy and the breast is well browned.
6. Serve immediately.

Golden Chicken Fries

Prep time: 20 minutes | Cook time: 6 minutes | Serves 4 to 6

- 1 pound (454 g) chicken tenders, cut into about ½-inch-wide strips
- Salt, to taste
- ¼ cup all-purpose flour
- 2 eggs
- ¾ cup panko bread crumbs
- ¾ cup crushed organic nacho
- cheese tortilla chips
- Cooking spray
- Seasonings:
- ½ teaspoon garlic powder
- 1 tablespoon chili powder
- ½ teaspoon onion powder
- 1 teaspoon ground cumin

1. Stir together all seasonings in a small bowl and set aside.
2. Sprinkle the chicken with salt. Place strips in a large bowl and sprinkle with 1 tablespoon of the seasoning mix. Stir well to distribute seasonings.
3. Add flour to chicken and stir well to coat all sides.
4. Beat eggs in a separate bowl.
5. In a shallow dish, combine the panko, crushed chips, and the remaining 2 teaspoons of seasoning mix.
6. Dip chicken strips in eggs, then roll in crumbs. Mist with oil or cooking spray. Arrange the chicken strips in a single layer in the basket.
7. Put the air fryer basket on the baking pan and slide into Rack Position 2, select Air Fry, set the temperature to 400ºF (205ºC) and set the time to 6 minutes.
8. After 4 minutes, remove from the oven. Flip the strips with tongs. Return to the oven and continue cooking.
9. When cooking is complete, the chicken should be crispy and its juices should be run clear.
10. Allow to cool under room temperature before serving.

Crispy Chicken Skin

Prep time: 5 minutes | Cook time: 6 minutes | Serves 4

- 1 pound (454 g) chicken skin, cut into slices
- 1 teaspoon melted butter
- ½ teaspoon crushed chili flakes
- 1 teaspoon dried dill
- Salt and ground black pepper, to taste

1. Combine all the ingredients in a large bowl. Toss to coat the chicken skin well.
2. Transfer the skin in the basket.
3. Put the air fryer basket on the baking pan and slide into Rack Position 2, select Air Fry, set temperature to 360ºF (182ºC) and set time to 6 minutes.
4. Stir the skin halfway through.
5. When cooking is complete, the skin should be crispy.
6. Serve immediately.

Chicken and Sweet Potato Curry

Prep time: 10 minutes | Cook time: 20 minutes | Serves 4

- 1 pound (454 g) boneless, skinless chicken thighs
- 1 teaspoon kosher salt, divided
- ¼ cup unsalted butter, melted
- 1 tablespoon curry powder
- 2 medium sweet potatoes, peeled and cut in 1-inch cubes
- 12 ounces (340 g) Brussels sprouts, halved

1. Sprinkle the chicken thighs with ½ teaspoon of kosher salt. Place them in the single layer in the baking pan.
2. In a small bowl, stir together the butter and curry powder.
3. Place the sweet potatoes and Brussels sprouts in a large bowl. Drizzle half the curry butter over the vegetables and add the remaining kosher salt. Toss to coat. Transfer the vegetables to the baking pan and place in a single layer around the chicken. Brush half of the remaining curry butter over the chicken.
4. Slide the baking pan into Rack Position 1, select Convection Bake, set temperature to 375ºF (190ºC), and set time to 20 minutes.
5. After 10 minutes, remove from the oven and turn over the chicken thighs. Baste them with the remaining curry butter. Return to the oven and continue cooking.
6. Cooking is complete when the sweet potatoes are tender and the chicken is cooked through and reads 165ºF (74ºC) on a meat thermometer.

Strawberry-Glazed Turkey

Prep time: 15 minutes | Cook time: 37 minutes | Serves 2

- 2 pounds (907 g) turkey breast
- 1 tablespoon olive oil
- Salt and ground black pepper, to taste
- 1 cup fresh strawberries

1. Rub the turkey bread with olive oil on a clean work surface, then sprinkle with salt and ground black pepper.
2. Transfer the turkey in the air fryer basket and spritz with cooking spray.
3. Put the air fryer basket on the baking pan and slide into Rack Position 2, select Air Fry, set temperature to 375ºF (190ºC) and set time to 30 minutes.
4. Flip the turkey breast halfway through.
5. Meanwhile, put the strawberries in a food processor and pulse until smooth.
6. When cooking is complete, spread the puréed strawberries over the turkey and fry for 7 more minutes.
7. Serve immediately.

Easy Cajun Chicken Drumsticks

Prep time: 5 minutes | Cook time: 18 minutes | Serves 5

- 1 tablespoon olive oil
- 10 chicken drumsticks
- 1½ tablespoons Cajun seasoning
- Salt and ground black pepper, to taste

1. Grease the basket with olive oil.
2. On a clean work surface, rub the chicken drumsticks with Cajun seasoning, salt, and ground black pepper.
3. Arrange the seasoned chicken drumsticks in the basket.
4. Put the air fryer basket on the baking pan and slide into Rack Position 2, select Air Fry, set temperature to 390ºF (199ºC) and set time to 18 minutes.
5. Flip the drumsticks halfway through.
6. When cooking is complete, the drumsticks should be lightly browned.
7. Remove the chicken drumsticks from the oven. Serve immediately.

Super Lemon Chicken

Prep time: 5 minutes | Cook time: 35 minutes | Serves 6

- 3 (8-ounce / 227-g) boneless, skinless chicken breasts, halved, rinsed
- 1 cup dried bread crumbs
- ¼ cup olive oil
- ¼ cup chicken broth
- Zest of 1 lemon
- 3 medium garlic cloves, minced
- ½ cup fresh lemon juice
- ½ cup water
- ¼ cup minced fresh oregano
- 1 medium lemon, cut into wedges
- ¼ cup minced fresh parsley, divided
- Cooking spray

1. Pour the bread crumbs in a shadow dish, then roll the chicken breasts in the bread crumbs to coat.
2. Spritz a skillet with cooking spray, and brown the coated chicken breasts over medium heat about 3 minutes on each side. Transfer the browned chicken to the baking pan.
3. In a small bowl, combine the remaining ingredients, except the lemon and parsley. Pour the sauce over the chicken.
4. Slide the baking pan into Rack Position 1, select Convection Bake, set the temperature to 325ºF (163ºC) and set the time to 30 minutes.
5. After 15 minutes, remove the pan from the oven. Flip the breasts. Return the pan to the oven and continue cooking.
6. When cooking is complete, the chicken should no longer pink.
7. Transfer to a serving platter, and spoon the sauce over the chicken. Garnish with the lemon and parsley.

Chapter 6 Meats

Air Fried Beef and Mushroom Stroganoff

Prep time: 15 minutes | Cook time: 14 minutes | Serves 4

- 1 pound (454 g) beef steak, thinly sliced
- 8 ounces (227 g) mushrooms, sliced
- 1 whole onion, chopped
- 2 cups beef broth
- 1 cup sour cream
- 4 tablespoons butter, melted
- 2 cups cooked egg noodles

1. Combine the mushrooms, onion, beef broth, sour cream and butter in a bowl until well blended. Add the beef steak to another bowl.
2. Spread the mushroom mixture over the steak and let marinate for 10 minutes.
3. Pour the marinated steak in the baking pan.
4. Slide the baking pan into Rack Position 1, select Convection Bake, set temperature to 400ºF (205ºC) and set time to 14 minutes.
5. Flip the steak halfway through the cooking time.
6. When cooking is complete, the steak should be browned and the vegetables should be tender.
7. Serve hot with the cooked egg noodles.

Air Fried London Broil

Prep time: 8 hours 5 minutes | Cook time: 25 minutes | Serves 6

- 2 tablespoons Worcestershire sauce
- 2 tablespoons minced onion
- ¼ cup honey
- ²/₃ cup ketchup
- 2 tablespoons apple cider vinegar
- ½ teaspoon paprika
- ¼ cup olive oil
- 1 teaspoon salt
- 1 teaspoon freshly ground black pepper
- 2 pounds (907 g) London broil, top round (about 1-inch thick)

1. Combine all the ingredients, except for the London broil, in a large bowl. Stir to mix well.
2. Pierce the meat with a fork generously on both sides, then dunk the meat in the mixture and press to coat well.
3. Wrap the bowl in plastic and refrigerate to marinate for at least 8 hours.
4. Discard the marinade and transfer the London broil to the basket.
5. Put the air fryer basket on the baking pan and slide into Rack Position 2, select Air Fry, set temperature to 400ºF (205ºC) and set time to 25 minutes.
6. Flip the meat halfway through the cooking time.
7. When cooking is complete, the meat should be well browned.
8. Transfer the cooked London broil on a plate and allow to cool for 5 minutes before slicing to serve.

Sumptuous Beef and Pork Sausage Meatloaf

Prep time: 10 minutes | Cook time: 25 minutes | Serves 4

- ¾ pound (340 g) ground chuck
- 4 ounces (113 g) ground pork sausage
- 2 eggs, beaten
- 1 cup Parmesan cheese, grated
- 1 cup chopped shallot
- 3 tablespoons plain milk
- 1 tablespoon oyster sauce
- 1 tablespoon fresh parsley
- 1 teaspoon garlic paste
- 1 teaspoon chopped porcini mushrooms
- ½ teaspoon cumin powder
- Seasoned salt and crushed red pepper flakes, to taste

1. In a large bowl, combine all the ingredients until well blended.
2. Place the meat mixture in the baking pan. Use a spatula to press the mixture to fill the pan.
3. Slide the baking pan into Rack Position 1, select Convection Bake, set temperature to 360ºF (182ºC) and set time to 25 minutes.
4. When cooking is complete, the meatloaf should be well browned.
5. Let the meatloaf rest for 5 minutes. Transfer to a serving dish and slice. Serve warm.

Beef Meatballs with Zesty Marinara Sauce

Prep time: 5 minutes | Cook time: 8 minutes | Serves 4

- 1 pound (454 g) lean ground sirloin beef
- 2 tablespoons seasoned bread crumbs
- ¼ teaspoon kosher salt
- 1 large egg, beaten
- 1 cup marinara sauce, for serving
- Cooking spray

1. Spritz the air fryer basket with cooking spray.
2. Mix all the ingredients, except for the marinara sauce, into a bowl until well blended. Shape the mixture into sixteen meatballs.
3. Arrange the meatballs in the prepared basket and mist with cooking spray.
4. Put the air fryer basket on the baking pan and slide into Rack Position 2, select Air Fry, set temperature to 360ºF (182ºC) and set time to 8 minutes.
5. Flip the meatballs halfway through.
6. When cooking is complete, the meatballs should be well browned.
7. Divide the meatballs among four plates and serve warm with the marinara sauce.

Tuscan Air Fried Veal Loin

Prep time: 1 hour 10 minutes | Cook time: 12 minutes | Makes 3 veal chops

- 1½ teaspoons crushed fennel seeds
- 1 tablespoon minced fresh rosemary leaves
- 1 tablespoon minced garlic
- 1½ teaspoons lemon zest
- 1½ teaspoons salt
- ½ teaspoon red pepper flakes
- 2 tablespoons olive oil
- 3 (10-ounce / 284-g) bone-in veal loin, about ½ inch thick

1. Combine all the ingredients, except for the veal loin, in a large bowl. Stir to mix well.
2. Dunk the loin in the mixture and press to submerge. Wrap the bowl in plastic and refrigerate for at least an hour to marinate.
3. Arrange the veal loin in the basket.
4. Put the air fryer basket on the baking pan and slide into Rack Position 2, select Air Fry, set temperature to 400ºF (205ºC) and set time to 12 minutes.
5. Flip the veal halfway through.
6. When cooking is complete, the internal temperature of the veal should reach at least 145ºF (63ºC) for medium rare.
7. Serve immediately.

Mushroom in Bacon-Wrapped Filets Mignons

Prep time: 10 minutes | Cook time: 13 minutes | Serves 8

- 1 ounce (28 g) dried porcini mushrooms
- ½ teaspoon granulated white sugar
- ½ teaspoon salt
- ½ teaspoon ground white pepper
- 8 (4-ounce / 113-g) filets mignons or beef tenderloin steaks
- 8 thin-cut bacon strips

1. Put the mushrooms, sugar, salt, and white pepper in a spice grinder and grind to combine.
2. On a clean work surface, rub the filets mignons with the mushroom mixture, then wrap each filet with a bacon strip. Secure with toothpicks if necessary.
3. Arrange the bacon-wrapped filets mignons in the basket, seam side down.
4. Put the air fryer basket on the baking pan and slide into Rack Position 2, select Air Fry, set temperature to 400ºF (205ºC) and set time to 13 minutes.
5. Flip the filets halfway through.
6. When cooking is complete, the filets should be medium rare.
7. Serve immediately.

Caraway Crusted Beef Steaks

Prep time: 5 minutes | Cook time: 10 minutes | Serves 4

- 4 beef steaks
- 2 teaspoons caraway seeds
- 2 teaspoons garlic powder
- Sea salt and cayenne pepper, to
- taste
- 1 tablespoon melted butter
- $1/_3$ cup almond flour
- 2 eggs, beaten

1. Add the beef steaks to a large bowl and toss with the caraway seeds, garlic powder, salt and pepper until well coated.
2. Stir together the melted butter and almond flour in a bowl. Whisk the eggs in a different bowl.
3. Dredge the seasoned steaks in the eggs, then dip in the almond and butter mixture.
4. Arrange the coated steaks in the basket.
5. Put the air fryer basket on the baking pan and slide into Rack Position 2, select Air Fry, set temperature to 355ºF (179ºC) and set time to 10 minutes.
6. Flip the steaks once halfway through to ensure even cooking.
7. When cooking is complete, the internal temperature of the beef steaks should reach at least 145ºF (63ºC) on a meat thermometer.
8. Transfer the steaks to plates. Let cool for 5 minutes and serve hot.

Easy Lamb Chops with Asparagus

Prep time: 10 minutes | Cook time: 15 minutes | Serves 4

- 4 asparagus spears, trimmed
- 2 tablespoons olive oil, divided
- 1 pound (454 g) lamb chops
- 1 garlic clove, minced
- 2 teaspoons chopped fresh thyme, for serving
- Salt and ground black pepper, to taste

1. Spritz the air fryer basket with cooking spray.
2. On a large plate, brush the asparagus with 1 tablespoon olive oil, then sprinkle with salt. Set aside.
3. On a separate plate, brush the lamb chops with remaining olive oil and sprinkle with salt and ground black pepper.
4. Arrange the lamb chops in the pan.
5. Put the air fryer basket on the baking pan and slide into Rack Position 2, select Air Fry, set temperature to 400ºF (205ºC) and set time to 15 minutes.
6. Flip the lamb chops and add the asparagus and garlic halfway through.
7. When cooking is complete, the lamb should be well browned and the asparagus should be tender.
8. Serve them on a plate with thyme on top.

Golden Lamb Chops

Prep time: 5 minutes | Cook time: 25 minutes | Serves 4

- 1 cup all-purpose flour
- 2 teaspoons dried sage leaves
- 2 teaspoons garlic powder
- 1 tablespoon mild paprika
- 1 tablespoon salt
- 4 (6-ounce / 170-g) bone-in lamb shoulder chops, fat trimmed
- Cooking spray

1. Spritz the air fryer basket with cooking spray.
2. Combine the flour, sage leaves, garlic powder, paprika, and salt in a large bowl. Stir to mix well. Dunk in the lamb chops and toss to coat well.
3. Arrange the lamb chops in the pan and spritz with cooking spray.
4. Put the air fryer basket on the baking pan and slide into Rack Position 2, select Air Fry, set temperature to 375ºF (190ºC) and set time to 25 minutes.
5. Flip the chops halfway through.
6. When cooking is complete, the chops should be golden brown and reaches your desired doneness.
7. Serve immediately.

Salsa Beef Meatballs

Prep time: 10 minutes | Cook time: 10 minutes | Serves 4

- 1 pound (454 g) ground beef (85% lean)
- ½ cup salsa
- ¼ cup diced green or red bell peppers
- 1 large egg, beaten
- ¼ cup chopped onions
- ½ teaspoon chili powder
- 1 clove garlic, minced
- ½ teaspoon ground cumin
- 1 teaspoon fine sea salt
- Lime wedges, for serving
- Cooking spray

1. Spritz the air fryer basket with cooking spray.
2. Combine all the ingredients in a large bowl. Stir to mix well.
3. Divide and shape the mixture into 1-inch balls. Arrange the balls in the pan and spritz with cooking spray.
4. Put the air fryer basket on the baking pan and slide into Rack Position 2, select Air Fry, set temperature to 350ºF (180ºC) and set time to 10 minutes.
5. Flip the balls with tongs halfway through.
6. When cooking is complete, the balls should be well browned.
7. Transfer the balls on a plate and squeeze the lime wedges over before serving.

Thai Curry Beef Meatballs

Prep time: 5 minutes | Cook time: 15 minutes | Serves 4

- 1 pound (454 g) ground beef
- 1 tablespoon sesame oil
- 2 teaspoons chopped lemongrass
- 1 teaspoon red Thai curry paste
- 1 teaspoon Thai seasoning blend
- Juice and zest of ½ lime
- Cooking spray

1. Spritz the air fryer basket with cooking spray.
2. In a medium bowl, combine all the ingredients until well blended.
3. Shape the meat mixture into 24 meatballs and arrange them in the pan.
4. Put the air fryer basket on the baking pan and slide into Rack Position 2, select Air Fry, set temperature to 380ºF (193ºC) and set time to 15 minutes.
5. Flip the meatballs halfway through.
6. When cooking is complete, the meatballs should be browned.
7. Transfer the meatballs to plates. Let cool for 5 minutes before serving.

Cinnamon-Beef Kofta

Prep time: 10 minutes | Cook time: 13 minutes | Makes 12 koftas

- 1½ pounds (680 g) lean ground beef
- 1 teaspoon onion powder
- ¾ teaspoon ground cinnamon
- ¾ teaspoon ground dried turmeric
- 1 teaspoon ground cumin
- ¾ teaspoon salt
- ¼ teaspoon cayenne
- 12 (3½- to 4-inch-long) cinnamon sticks
- Cooking spray

1. Spritz the air fryer basket with cooking spray.
2. Combine all the ingredients, except for the cinnamon sticks, in a large bowl. Toss to mix well.
3. Divide and shape the mixture into 12 balls, then wrap each ball around each cinnamon stick and leave a quarter of the length uncovered.
4. Arrange the beef-cinnamon sticks in the prepared pan and spritz with cooking spray.
5. Put the air fryer basket on the baking pan and slide into Rack Position 2, select Air Fry, set temperature to 375ºF (190ºC) and set time to 13 minutes.
6. Flip the sticks halfway through the cooking.
7. When cooking is complete, the beef should be browned.
8. Serve immediately.

Air Fried Golden Wasabi Spam

Prep time: 5 minutes | Cook time: 12 minutes | Serves 3

- ²/₃ cup all-purpose flour
- 2 large eggs
- 1½ tablespoons wasabi paste
- 2 cups panko bread crumbs
- 6 ½-inch-thick spam slices
- Cooking spray

1. Spritz the air fryer basket with cooking spray.
2. Pour the flour in a shallow plate. Whisk the eggs with wasabi in a large bowl. Pour the panko in a separate shallow plate.
3. Dredge the spam slices in the flour first, then dunk in the egg mixture, and then roll the spam over the panko to coat well. Shake the excess off.
4. Arrange the spam slices in the pan and spritz with cooking spray.
5. Put the air fryer basket on the baking pan and slide into Rack Position 2, select Air Fry, set temperature to 400ºF (205ºC) and set time to 12 minutes.
6. Flip the spam slices halfway through.
7. When cooking is complete, the spam slices should be golden and crispy.
8. Serve immediately.

Bacon-Wrapped Hot Dogs with Mayo-Ketchup Sauce

Prep time: 5 minutes | Cook time: 10 minutes | Serves 5

- 10 thin slices of bacon
- 5 pork hot dogs, halved
- 1 teaspoon cayenne pepper
- Sauce:
- ¼ cup mayonnaise
- 4 tablespoons low-carb ketchup
- 1 teaspoon rice vinegar
- 1 teaspoon chili powder

1. Arrange the slices of bacon on a clean work surface. One by one, place the halved hot dog on one end of each slice, season with cayenne pepper and wrap the hot dog with the bacon slices and secure with toothpicks as needed.
2. Place wrapped hot dogs in the basket.
3. Put the air fryer basket on the baking pan and slide into Rack Position 2, select Air Fry, set temperature to 390ºF (199ºC) and set time to 10 minutes.
4. Flip the bacon-wrapped hot dogs halfway through.
5. When cooking is complete, the bacon should be crispy and browned.
6. Make the sauce: Stir all the ingredients for the sauce in a small bowl. Wrap the bowl in plastic and set in the refrigerator until ready to serve.
7. Transfer the hot dogs to a platter and serve hot with the sauce.

Kielbasa Sausage with Pineapple and Bell Peppers

Prep time: 15 minutes | Cook time: 10 minutes | Serves 2 to 4

- ¾ pound (340 g) kielbasa sausage, cut into ½-inch slices
- 1 (8-ounce / 227-g) can pineapple chunks in juice, drained
- 1 cup bell pepper chunks
- 1 tablespoon barbecue seasoning
- 1 tablespoon soy sauce
- Cooking spray

1. Spritz the air fryer basket with cooking spray.
2. Combine all the ingredients in a large bowl. Toss to mix well.
3. Pour the sausage mixture in the basket.
4. Put the air fryer basket on the baking pan and slide into Rack Position 2, select Air Fry, set temperature to 390ºF (199ºC) and set time to 10 minutes.
5. After 5 minutes, remove from the oven. Stir the sausage mixture. Return to the oven and continue cooking.
6. When cooking is complete, the sausage should be lightly browned and the bell pepper and pineapple should be soft.
7. Serve immediately.

Lechon Kawali

Prep time: 10 minutes | Cook time: 30 minutes | Serves 4

- 1 pound (454 g) pork belly, cut into three thick chunks
- 6 garlic cloves
- 2 bay leaves
- 2 tablespoons soy sauce
- 1 teaspoon kosher salt
- 1 teaspoon ground black pepper
- 3 cups water
- Cooking spray

1. Put all the ingredients in a pressure cooker, then put the lid on and cook on high for 15 minutes.
2. Natural release the pressure and release any remaining pressure, transfer the tender pork belly on a clean work surface. Allow to cool under room temperature until you can handle.
3. Generously Spritz the air fryer basket with cooking spray.
4. Cut each chunk into two slices, then put the pork slices in the pan.
5. Put the air fryer basket on the baking pan and slide into Rack Position 2, select Air Fry, set temperature to 400ºF (205ºC) and set time to 15 minutes.
6. After 7 minutes, remove from the oven. Flip the pork. Return to the oven and continue cooking.
7. When cooking is complete, the pork fat should be crispy.
8. Serve immediately.

Italian Sausages and Red Grapes

Prep time: 10 minutes | Cook time: 20 minutes | Serves 6

- 2 pounds (905 g) seedless red grapes
- 3 shallots, sliced
- 2 teaspoons fresh thyme
- 2 tablespoons olive oil
- ½ teaspoon kosher salt
- Freshly ground black pepper, to taste
- 6 links (about 1½ pounds / 680 g) hot Italian sausage
- 3 tablespoons balsamic vinegar

1. Place the grapes in a large bowl. Add the shallots, thyme, olive oil, salt, and pepper. Gently toss. Place the grapes in the baking pan. Arrange the sausage links evenly in the pan.
2. Slide the baking pan into Rack Position 1, select Convection Bake, set temperature to 375ºF (190ºC), and set time to 20 minutes.
3. After 10 minutes, remove the pan. Turn over the sausages and sprinkle the vinegar over the sausages and grapes. Gently toss the grapes and move them to one side of the pan. Return the pan to the oven and continue cooking.
4. When cooking is complete, the grapes should be very soft and the sausages browned. Serve immediately.

Ravioli with Beef-Marinara Sauce

Prep time: 10 minutes | Cook time: 10 minutes | Serves 4

- 1 (20-ounce / 567-g) package frozen cheese ravioli
- 1 teaspoon kosher salt
- 1¼ cups water
- 6 ounces (170 g) cooked ground beef
- 2½ cups Marinara sauce
- ¼ cup grated Parmesan cheese, for garnish

1. Place the ravioli in an even layer in the baking pan. Stir the salt into the water until dissolved and pour it over the ravioli.
2. Slide the baking pan into Rack Position 1, select Convection Bake, set temperature to 450ºF (235ºC), and set time to 10 minutes.
3. While the ravioli is cooking, mix the ground beef into the marinara sauce in a medium bowl.
4. After 6 minutes, remove the pan from the oven. Blot off any remaining water, or drain the ravioli and return them to the pan. Pour the meat sauce over the ravioli. Return the pan to the oven and continue cooking.
5. When cooking is complete, the ravioli should be tender and sauce heated through. Gently stir the ingredients. Serve the ravioli with the Parmesan cheese, if desired.

Crispy Pork Tenderloin

Prep time: 5 minutes | Cook time: 10 minutes | Serves 6

- 2 large egg whites
- 1½ tablespoons Dijon mustard
- 2 cups crushed pretzel crumbs
- 1½ pounds (680 g) pork tenderloin, cut into ¼-pound (113-g) sections
- Cooking spray

1. Spritz the air fryer basket with cooking spray.
2. Whisk the egg whites with Dijon mustard in a bowl until bubbly. Pour the pretzel crumbs in a separate bowl.
3. Dredge the pork tenderloin in the egg white mixture and press to coat. Shake the excess off and roll the tenderloin over the pretzel crumbs.
4. Arrange the well-coated pork tenderloin in the pan and spritz with cooking spray.
5. Put the air fryer basket on the baking pan and slide into Rack Position 2, select Air Fry, set temperature to 350ºF (180ºC) and set time to 10 minutes.
6. After 5 minutes, remove from the oven. Flip the pork. Return to the oven and continue cooking.
7. When cooking is complete, the pork should be golden brown and crispy.
8. Serve immediately.

Easy Pork Chop Roast

Prep time: 5 minutes | Cook time: 20 minutes | Serves 2

- 2 (10-ounce / 284-g) bone-in, center cut pork chops, 1-inch thick
- 2 teaspoons Worcestershire sauce
- Salt and ground black pepper, to taste
- Cooking spray

1. Rub the Worcestershire sauce on both sides of pork chops.
2. Season with salt and pepper to taste.
3. Spritz the baking pan with cooking spray and place the chops in the pan side by side.
4. Slide the baking pan into Rack Position 1, select Convection Bake, set the temperature to 350ºF (180ºC) and set the time to 20 minutes.
5. After 10 minutes, remove from the oven. Flip the pork chops with tongs. Return to the oven and continue cooking.
6. When cooking is complete, the pork should be well browned on both sides.
7. Let rest for 5 minutes before serving.

Chapter 7
Appetizers and Snacks

Parmesan Cauliflower

Prep time: 15 minutes | Cook time: 15 minutes | Makes 5 cups

- 8 cups small cauliflower florets (about 1¼ pounds / 567 g)
- 3 tablespoons olive oil
- 1 teaspoon garlic powder
- ½ teaspoon salt
- ½ teaspoon turmeric
- ¼ cup shredded Parmesan cheese

1. In a bowl, combine the cauliflower florets, olive oil, garlic powder, salt, and turmeric and toss to coat. Transfer to the air fryer basket.
2. Put the air fryer basket on the baking pan and slide into Rack Position 2, select Air Fry, set temperature to 390ºF (199ºC), and set time to 15 minutes.
3. After 5 minutes, remove from the oven and stir the cauliflower florets. Return to the oven and continue cooking.
4. After 6 minutes, remove from the oven and stir the cauliflower. Return to the oven and continue cooking for 4 minutes. The cauliflower florets should be crisp-tender.
5. When cooking is complete, remove from the oven to a plate. Sprinkle with the shredded Parmesan cheese and toss well. Serve warm.

Crunchy Parmesan Snack Mix

Prep time: 5 minutes | Cook time: 6 minutes | Makes 6 cups

- 2 cups oyster crackers
- 2 cups Chex rice
- 1 cup sesame sticks
- ⅔ cup finely grated Parmesan cheese
- 8 tablespoons unsalted butter, melted
- 1½ teaspoons granulated garlic
- ½ teaspoon kosher salt

1. Toss together all the ingredients in a large bowl until well coated. Spread the mixture in the baking pan in an even layer.
2. Slide the baking pan into Rack Position 1, select Convection Bake, set temperature to 350ºF (180ºC) and set time to 6 minutes.
3. After 3 minutes, remove from the oven and stir the mixture. Return to the oven and continue cooking.
4. When cooking is complete, the mixture should be lightly browned and fragrant. Let cool before serving.

Cheesy Jalapeño Poppers

Prep time: 10 minutes | Cook time: 15 minutes | Serves 8

- 6 ounces (170 g) cream cheese, at room temperature
- 4 ounces (113 g) shredded Cheddar cheese
- 1 teaspoon chili powder
- 12 large jalapeño peppers,

- deseeded and sliced in half lengthwise
- 2 slices cooked bacon, chopped
- ¼ cup panko bread crumbs
- 1 tablespoon butter, melted

1. In a medium bowl, whisk together the cream cheese, Cheddar cheese and chili powder. Spoon the cheese mixture into the jalapeño halves and arrange them in the baking pan.
2. In a small bowl, stir together the bacon, bread crumbs and butter. Sprinkle the mixture over the jalapeño halves.
3. Slide the baking pan into Rack Position 1, select Convection Bake, set temperature to 375ºF (190ºC) and set time to 15 minutes.
4. When cooking is complete, remove from the oven. Let the poppers cool for 5 minutes before serving.

Salty Baked Almonds

Prep time: 5 minutes | Cook time: 25 minutes | Serves 4

- 1 cup raw almonds
- 1 egg white, beaten

- ½ teaspoon coarse sea salt

1. Spread the almonds in the baking pan in an even layer.
2. Slide the baking pan into Rack Position 1, select Convection Bake, set temperature to 350ºF (180ºC) and set time to 20 minutes.
3. When cooking is complete, the almonds should be lightly browned and fragrant. Remove from the oven.
4. Coat the almonds with the egg white and sprinkle with the salt. Return the pan to the oven.
5. Slide the baking pan into Rack Position 1, select Convection Bake, set temperature to 350ºF (180ºC) and set time to 5 minutes.
6. When cooking is complete, the almonds should be dried. Cool completely before serving.

Spicy and Sweet Nuts

Prep time: 5 minutes | Cook time: 15 minutes | Makes 4 cups

- 1 pound (454 g) walnut halves and pieces
- ½ cup granulated sugar
- 3 tablespoons vegetable oil
- 1 teaspoon cayenne pepper
- ½ teaspoon fine salt

1. Soak the walnuts in a large bowl with boiling water for a minute or two. Drain the walnuts. Stir in the sugar, oil and cayenne pepper to coat well. Spread the walnuts in a single layer in the baking pan.
2. Slide the baking pan into Rack Position 1, select Convection Bake, set temperature to 325ºF (163ºC) and set time to 15 minutes.
3. After 7 or 8 minutes, remove from the oven. Stir the nuts. Return the pan to the oven and continue cooking, check frequently.
4. When cooking is complete, the walnuts should be dark golden brown. Remove from the oven. Sprinkle the nuts with the salt and let cool. Serve warm.

Sausage Balls with Cheese

Prep time: 10 minutes | Cook time: 10 minutes | Serves 8

- 12 ounces (340 g) mild ground sausage
- 1½ cups baking mix
- 1 cup shredded mild Cheddar
- cheese
- 3 ounces (85 g) cream cheese, at room temperature
- 1 to 2 tablespoons olive oil

1. Line the air fryer basket with parchment paper. Set aside.
2. Mix together the ground sausage, baking mix, Cheddar cheese, and cream cheese in a large bowl and stir to incorporate.
3. Divide the sausage mixture into 16 equal portions and roll them into 1-inch balls with your hands. Arrange the sausage balls on the parchment, leaving space between each ball. Brush the sausage balls with the olive oil.
4. Put the air fryer basket on the baking pan and slide into Rack Position 2, select Air Fry, set temperature to 325ºF (163ºC), and set time to 10 minutes.
5. Flip the balls halfway through the cooking time.
6. When cooking is complete, the balls should be firm and lightly browned on both sides. Remove from the oven to a plate and serve warm.

Crispy Cinnamon Apple Chips

Prep time: 10 minutes | Cook time: 10 minutes | Serves 4

- 2 apples, cored and cut into thin slices
- 2 heaped teaspoons ground cinnamon
- Cooking spray

1. Spritz the air fryer basket with cooking spray.
2. In a medium bowl, sprinkle the apple slices with the cinnamon. Toss until evenly coated. Spread the coated apple slices on the pan in a single layer.
3. Put the air fryer basket on the baking pan and slide into Rack Position 2, select Air Fry, set temperature to 350°F (180°C) and set time to 10 minutes.
4. After 5 minutes, remove from the oven. Stir the apple slices and return to the oven to continue cooking.
5. When cooking is complete, the slices should be until crispy. Remove from the oven and let rest for 5 minutes before serving.

Browned Ricotta with Capers and Lemon

Prep time: 10 minutes | Cook time: 8 minutes | Serves 4 to 6

- 1½ cups whole milk ricotta cheese
- 2 tablespoons extra-virgin olive oil
- 2 tablespoons capers, rinsed
- Zest of 1 lemon, plus more for garnish
- 1 teaspoon finely chopped fresh rosemary
- Pinch crushed red pepper flakes
- Salt and freshly ground black pepper, to taste
- 1 tablespoon grated Parmesan cheese

1. In a mixing bowl, stir together the ricotta cheese, olive oil, capers, lemon zest, rosemary, red pepper flakes, salt, and pepper until well combined.
2. Spread the mixture evenly in the baking pan.
3. Slide the baking pan into Rack Position 2, select Air Fry, set temperature to 380°F (193°C), and set time to 8 minutes.
4. When cooking is complete, the top should be nicely browned. Remove from the oven and top with a sprinkle of grated Parmesan cheese. Garnish with the lemon zest and serve warm.

Spicy Tortilla Chips

Prep time: 5 minutes | Cook time: 5 minutes | Serves 4

- ½ teaspoon ground cumin
- ½ teaspoon paprika
- ½ teaspoon chili powder
- ½ teaspoon salt
- Pinch cayenne pepper
- 8 (6-inch) corn tortillas, each cut into 6 wedges
- Cooking spray

1. Lightly spritz the air fryer basket with cooking spray.
2. Stir together the cumin, paprika, chili powder, salt, and pepper in a small bowl.
3. Place the tortilla wedges in the basket in a single layer. Lightly mist them with cooking spray. Sprinkle the seasoning mixture on top of the tortilla wedges.
4. Put the air fryer basket on the baking pan and slide into Rack Position 2, select Air Fry, set temperature to 375ºF (190ºC), and set time to 5 minutes.
5. Stir the tortilla wedges halfway through the cooking time.
6. When cooking is complete, the chips should be lightly browned and crunchy. Remove from the oven. Let the tortilla chips cool for 5 minutes and serve.

Broiled Prosciutto-Wrapped Pears

Prep time: 12 minutes | Cook time: 6 minutes | Serves 8

- 2 large, ripe Anjou pears
- 4 thin slices Parma prosciutto
- 2 teaspoons aged balsamic vinegar

1. Peel the pears. Slice into 8 wedges and cut out the core from each wedge.
2. Cut the prosciutto into 8 long strips. Wrap each pear wedge with a strip of prosciutto. Place the wrapped pears in the air fryer basket.
3. Put the air fryer basket on the baking pan and slide into Rack Position 2, select Convection Broil, set temperature to High and set time to 6 minutes.
4. After 2 or 3 minutes, check the pears. The pears should be turned over if the prosciutto is beginning to crisp up and brown. Return to the oven and continue cooking.
5. When cooking is complete, remove from the oven. Drizzle the pears with the balsamic vinegar and serve warm.

Chapter 8 Desserts

Classic Pound Cake

Prep time: 5 minutes | Cook time: 30 minutes | Serves 8

- 1 stick butter, at room temperature
- 1 cup Swerve
- 4 eggs
- 1½ cups coconut flour
- ½ cup buttermilk
- ½ teaspoon baking soda
- ½ teaspoon baking powder
- ¼ teaspoon salt
- 1 teaspoon vanilla essence
- A pinch of ground star anise
- A pinch of freshly grated nutmeg
- Cooking spray

1. Spray the baking pan with cooking spray.
2. With an electric mixer or hand mixer, beat the butter and Swerve until creamy. One at a time, mix in the eggs and whisk until fluffy. Add the remaining ingredients and stir to combine.
3. Transfer the batter to the prepared baking pan.
4. Slide the baking pan into Rack Position 1, select Convection Bake, set temperature to 320ºF (160ºC), and set time to 30 minutes.
5. When cooking is complete, the center of the cake should be springy.
6. Allow the cake to cool in the pan for 10 minutes before removing and serving.

Blackberry Chocolate Cake

Prep time: 10 minutes | Cook time: 22 minutes | Serves 8

- ½ cup butter, at room temperature
- 2 ounces (57 g) Swerve
- 4 eggs
- 1 cup almond flour
- 1 teaspoon baking soda
- $1/3$ teaspoon baking powder
- ½ cup cocoa powder
- 1 teaspoon orange zest
- $1/3$ cup fresh blackberries

1. With an electric mixer or hand mixer, beat the butter and Swerve until creamy.
2. One at a time, mix in the eggs and beat again until fluffy.
3. Add the almond flour, baking soda, baking powder, cocoa powder, orange zest and mix well. Add the butter mixture to the almond flour mixture and stir until well blended. Fold in the blackberries.
4. Scrape the batter into the baking pan.
5. Slide the baking pan into Rack Position 1, select Convection Bake, set temperature to 335ºF (168ºC), and set time to 22 minutes.
6. When cooking is complete, a toothpick inserted into the center of the cake should come out clean.
7. Allow the cake cool on a wire rack to room temperature. Serve immediately.

Lemon-Raspberry Muffins

Prep time: 5 minutes | Cook time: 15 minutes | Serves 6

- 2 cups almond flour
- ¾ cup Swerve
- 1¼ teaspoons baking powder
- $1/_3$ teaspoon ground allspice
- $1/_3$ teaspoon ground anise star
- ½ teaspoon grated lemon zest
- ¼ teaspoon salt
- 2 eggs
- 1 cup sour cream
- ½ cup coconut oil
- ½ cup raspberries

1. Line a muffin pan with 6 paper liners.
2. In a mixing bowl, mix the almond flour, Swerve, baking powder, allspice, anise, lemon zest, and salt.
3. In another mixing bowl, beat the eggs, sour cream, and coconut oil until well mixed. Add the egg mixture to the flour mixture and stir to combine. Mix in the raspberries.
4. Scrape the batter into the prepared muffin cups, filling each about three-quarters full.
5. Put the muffin pan into Rack Position 1, select Convection Bake, set temperature to 345ºF (174ºC), and set time to 15 minutes.
6. When cooking is complete, the tops should be golden and a toothpick inserted in the middle should come out clean.
7. Allow the muffins to cool for 10 minutes in the muffin pan before removing and serving.

Coconut Pineapple Sticks

Prep time: 10 minutes | Cook time: 10 minutes | Serves 4

- ½ fresh pineapple, cut into sticks
- ¼ cup desiccated coconut

1. Place the desiccated coconut on a plate and roll the pineapple sticks in the coconut until well coated.
2. Lay the pineapple sticks in the air fryer basket.
3. Put the air fryer basket on the baking pan and slide into Rack Position 2, select Air Fry, set temperature to 400ºF (205ºC), and set time to 10 minutes.
4. When cooking is complete, the pineapple sticks should be crisp-tender.
5. Serve warm.

Vanilla Walnuts Tart

Prep time: 5 minutes | Cook time: 13 minutes | Serves 6

- 1 cup coconut milk
- ½ cup walnuts, ground
- ½ cup Swerve
- ½ cup almond flour
- ½ stick butter, at room temperature
- 2 eggs
- 1 teaspoon vanilla essence
- ¼ teaspoon ground cardamom
- ¼ teaspoon ground cloves
- Cooking spray

1. Coat the baking pan with cooking spray.
2. Combine all the ingredients except the oil in a large bowl and stir until well blended. Spoon the batter mixture into the baking pan.
3. Slide the baking pan into Rack Position 1, select Convection Bake, set temperature to 360ºF (182ºC), and set time to 13 minutes.
4. When cooking is complete, a toothpick inserted into the center of the tart should come out clean.
5. Remove from the oven and place on a wire rack to cool. Serve immediately.

Apple-Peach Crisp with Oatmeal

Prep time: 10 minutes | Cook time: 10 to 12 minutes | Serves 4

- 2 peaches, peeled, pitted, and chopped
- 1 apple, peeled and chopped
- 2 tablespoons honey
- 3 tablespoons packed brown sugar
- 2 tablespoons unsalted butter, at room temperature
- ½ cup quick-cooking oatmeal
- ⅓ cup whole-wheat pastry flour
- ½ teaspoon ground cinnamon

1. Place the peaches, apple, and honey in the baking pan and toss until thoroughly combined.
2. Mix together the brown sugar, butter, oatmeal, pastry flour, and cinnamon in a medium bowl and stir until crumbly. Sprinkle this mixture generously on top of the peaches and apples.
3. Slide the baking pan into Rack Position 1, select Convection Bake, set temperature to 380ºF (193ºC), and set the time to 10 minutes.
4. Bake until the fruit is bubbling and the topping is golden brown.
5. Once cooking is complete, remove from the oven and allow to cool for 5 minutes before serving.

Peanut Butter-Chocolate Bread Pudding

Prep time: 10 minutes | Cook time: 10 minutes | Serves 8

- 1 egg
- 1 egg yolk
- ¾ cup chocolate milk
- 3 tablespoons brown sugar
- 3 tablespoons peanut butter
- 2 tablespoons cocoa powder
- 1 teaspoon vanilla
- 5 slices firm white bread, cubed
- Nonstick cooking spray

1. Spritz the baking pan with nonstick cooking spray.
2. Whisk together the egg, egg yolk, chocolate milk, brown sugar, peanut butter, cocoa powder, and vanilla until well combined.
3. Fold in the bread cubes and stir to mix well. Allow the bread soak for 10 minutes.
4. When ready, transfer the egg mixture to the prepared baking pan.
5. Slide the baking pan into Rack Position 1, select Convection Bake, set temperature to 330ºF (166ºC), and set time to 10 minutes.
6. When done, the pudding should be just firm to the touch.
7. Serve at room temperature.

Chocolate and Coconut Cake

Prep time: 5 minutes | Cook time: 15 minutes | Serves 6

- ½ cup unsweetened chocolate, chopped
- ½ stick butter, at room temperature
- 1 tablespoon liquid stevia
- 1½ cups coconut flour
- 2 eggs, whisked
- ½ teaspoon vanilla extract
- A pinch of fine sea salt
- Cooking spray

1. Place the chocolate, butter, and stevia in a microwave-safe bowl. Microwave for about 30 seconds until melted.
2. Let the chocolate mixture cool for 5 to 10 minutes.
3. Add the remaining ingredients to the bowl of chocolate mixture and whisk to incorporate.
4. Lightly spray the baking pan with cooking spray.
5. Scrape the chocolate mixture into the prepared baking pan.
6. Slide the baking pan into Rack Position 1, select Convection Bake, set temperature to 330ºF (166ºC), and set time to 15 minutes.
7. When cooking is complete, the top should spring back lightly when gently pressed with your fingers.
8. Let the cake cool for 5 minutes and serve.

Crispy Pineapple Rings

Prep time: 5 minutes | Cook time: 7 minutes | Serves 6

- 1 cup rice milk
- ²/₃ cup flour
- ½ cup water
- ¼ cup unsweetened flaked coconut
- 4 tablespoons sugar
- ½ teaspoon baking soda
- ½ teaspoon baking powder
- ½ teaspoon vanilla essence
- ½ teaspoon ground cinnamon
- ¼ teaspoon ground anise star
- Pinch of kosher salt
- 1 medium pineapple, peeled and sliced

1. In a large bowl, stir together all the ingredients except the pineapple.
2. Dip each pineapple slice into the batter until evenly coated.
3. Arrange the pineapple slices in the air fryer basket.
4. Put the air fryer basket on the baking pan and slide into Rack Position 2, select Air Fry, set temperature to 380ºF (193ºC), and set time to 7 minutes.
5. When cooking is complete, the pineapple rings should be golden brown.
6. Remove from the oven to a plate and cool for 5 minutes before serving.

Chocolate Cheesecake

Prep time: 5 minutes | Cook time: 18 minutes | Serves 6

Crust:
- ½ cup butter, melted
- ½ cup coconut flour
- 2 tablespoons stevia
- Cooking spray

Topping:
- 4 ounces (113 g) unsweetened baker's chocolate
- 1 cup mascarpone cheese, at room
- temperature
- 1 teaspoon vanilla extract
- 2 drops peppermint extract

1. Lightly coat the baking pan with cooking spray.
2. In a mixing bowl, whisk together the butter, flour, and stevia until well combined. Transfer the mixture to the prepared baking pan.
3. Slide the baking pan into Rack Position 1, select Convection Bake, set temperature to 350ºF (180ºC), and set time to 18 minutes.
4. When done, a toothpick inserted in the center should come out clean.
5. Remove the crust from the oven to a wire rack to cool.
6. Once cooled completely, place it in the freezer for 20 minutes.
7. When ready, combine all the ingredients for the topping in a small bowl and stir to incorporate.
8. Spread this topping over the crust and let it sit for another 15 minutes in the freezer.
9. Serve chilled.

Chapter 9
Casseroles, Frittata, and Quiche

Riced Cauliflower Casserole

Prep time: 8 minutes | Cook time: 12 minutes | Serves 4

- 1 head cauliflower, cut into florets
- 1 cup okra, chopped
- 1 yellow bell pepper, chopped
- 2 eggs, beaten
- ½ cup chopped onion
- 1 tablespoon soy sauce
- 2 tablespoons olive oil
- Salt and ground black pepper, to taste

1. Spritz the baking pan with cooking spray.
2. Put the cauliflower in a food processor and pulse to rice the cauliflower.
3. Pour the cauliflower rice in the baking pan and add the remaining ingredients. Stir to mix well.
4. Slide the baking pan into Rack Position 1, select Convection Bake, set temperature to 380ºF (193ºC) and set time to 12 minutes.
5. When cooking is complete, the eggs should be set.
6. Remove from the oven and serve immediately.

Easy Corn and Bell Pepper Casserole

Prep time: 10 minutes | Cook time: 20 minutes | Serves 4

- 1 cup corn kernels
- ¼ cup bell pepper, finely chopped
- ½ cup low-fat milk
- 1 large egg, beaten
- ½ cup yellow cornmeal
- ½ cup all-purpose flour
- ½ teaspoon baking powder
- 2 tablespoons melted unsalted butter
- 1 tablespoon granulated sugar
- Pinch of cayenne pepper
- ¼ teaspoon kosher salt
- Cooking spray

1. Spritz the baking pan with cooking spray.
2. Combine all the ingredients in a large bowl. Stir to mix well. Pour the mixture into the baking pan.
3. Slide the baking pan into Rack Position 1, select Convection Bake, set temperature to 330ºF (166ºC) and set time to 20 minutes.
4. When cooking is complete, the casserole should be lightly browned and set.
5. Remove from the oven and serve immediately.

Hillbilly Broccoli Cheese Casserole

Prep time: 5 minutes | Cook time: 30 minutes | Serves 6

- 4 cups broccoli florets
- ¼ cup heavy whipping cream
- ½ cup sharp Cheddar cheese, shredded
- ¼ cup ranch dressing
- Kosher salt and ground black pepper, to taste

1. Combine all the ingredients in a large bowl. Toss to coat well broccoli well.
2. Pour the mixture into the baking pan.
3. Slide the baking pan into Rack Position 1, select Convection Bake, set temperature to 375ºF (190ºC) and set time to 30 minutes.
4. When cooking is complete, the broccoli should be tender.
5. Remove the baking pan from the oven and serve immediately.

Ritzy Pimento and Almond Turkey Casserole

Prep time: 5 minutes | Cook time: 32 minutes | Serves 4

- 1 pound (454 g) turkey breasts
- 1 tablespoon olive oil
- 2 boiled eggs, chopped
- 2 tablespoons chopped pimentos
- ¼ cup slivered almonds, chopped
- ¼ cup mayonnaise
- ½ cup diced celery
- 2 tablespoons chopped green onion
- ¼ cup cream of chicken soup
- ¼ cup bread crumbs
- Salt and ground black pepper, to taste

1. Put the turkey breasts in a large bowl. Sprinkle with salt and ground black pepper and drizzle with olive oil. Toss to coat well.
2. Transfer the turkey to the air fryer basket.
3. Put the air fryer basket on the baking pan and slide into Rack Position 2, select Air Fry, set temperature to 390ºF (199ºC) and set time to 12 minutes.
4. Flip the turkey halfway through.
5. When cooking is complete, the turkey should be well browned.
6. Remove the turkey breasts from the oven and cut into cubes, then combine the chicken cubes with eggs, pimentos, almonds, mayo, celery, green onions, and chicken soup in a large bowl. Stir to mix.
7. Pour the mixture into the baking pan, then spread with bread crumbs.
8. Slide the baking pan into Rack Position 1, select Convection Bake, set time to 20 minutes.
9. When cooking is complete, the eggs should be set.
10. Remove from the oven and serve immediately.

Taco Beef and Chile Casserole

Prep time: 10 minutes | Cook time: 15 minutes | Serves 4

- 1 pound (454 g) 85% lean ground beef
- 1 tablespoon taco seasoning
- 1 (7-ounce / 198-g) can diced mild green chiles
- ½ cup milk
- 2 large eggs
- 1 cup shredded Mexican cheese blend
- 2 tablespoons all-purpose flour
- ½ teaspoon kosher salt
- Cooking spray

1. Spritz the baking pan with cooking spray.
2. Toss the ground beef with taco seasoning in a large bowl to mix well. Pour the seasoned ground beef in the prepared baking pan.
3. Combing the remaining ingredients in a medium bowl. Whisk to mix well, then pour the mixture over the ground beef.
4. Slide the baking pan into Rack Position 1, select Convection Bake, set temperature to 350ºF (180ºC) and set time to 15 minutes.
5. When cooking is complete, a toothpick inserted in the center should come out clean.
6. Remove the casserole from the oven and allow to cool for 5 minutes, then slice to serve.

Pastrami Casserole

Prep time: 10 minutes | Cook time: 8 minutes | Serves 2

- 1 cup pastrami, sliced
- 1 bell pepper, chopped
- ¼ cup Greek yogurt
- 2 spring onions, chopped
- ½ cup Cheddar cheese, grated
- 4 eggs
- ¼ teaspoon ground black pepper
- Sea salt, to taste
- Cooking spray

1. Spritz the baking pan with cooking spray.
2. Whisk together all the ingredients in a large bowl. Stir to mix well. Pour the mixture into the baking pan.
3. Slide the baking pan into Rack Position 1, select Convection Bake, set temperature to 330ºF (166ºC) and set time to 8 minutes.
4. When cooking is complete, the eggs should be set and the casserole edges should be lightly browned.
5. Remove from the oven and allow to cool for 10 minutes before serving.

Sausage and Colorful Peppers Casserole

Prep time: 15 minutes | Cook time: 25 minutes | Serves 6

- 1 pound (454 g) minced breakfast sausage
- 1 yellow pepper, diced
- 1 red pepper, diced
- 1 green pepper, diced
- 1 sweet onion, diced
- 2 cups Cheddar cheese, shredded
- 6 eggs
- Salt and freshly ground black pepper, to taste
- Fresh parsley, for garnish

1. Cook the sausage in a nonstick skillet over medium heat for 10 minutes or until well browned. Stir constantly.
2. When the cooking is finished, transfer the cooked sausage to the baking pan and add the peppers and onion. Scatter with Cheddar cheese.
3. Whisk the eggs with salt and ground black pepper in a large bowl, then pour the mixture into the baking pan.
4. Slide the baking pan into Rack Position 1, select Convection Bake, set temperature to 360ºF (182ºC) and set time to 15 minutes.
5. When cooking is complete, the egg should be set and the edges of the casserole should be lightly browned.
6. Remove from the oven and top with fresh parsley before serving.

Shrimp Spinach Frittata

Prep time: 6 minutes | Cook time: 14 minutes | Serves 4

- 4 whole eggs
- 1 teaspoon dried basil
- ½ cup shrimp, cooked and chopped
- ½ cup baby spinach
- ½ cup rice, cooked
- ½ cup Monterey Jack cheese, grated
- Salt, to taste
- Cooking spray

1. Spritz the baking pan with cooking spray.
2. Whisk the eggs with basil and salt in a large bowl until bubbly, then mix in the shrimp, spinach, rice, and cheese.
3. Pour the mixture into the baking pan.
4. Slide the baking pan into Rack Position 1, select Convection Bake, set temperature to 360ºF (182ºC) and set time to 14 minutes.
5. Stir the mixture halfway through.
6. When cooking is complete, the eggs should be set and the frittata should be golden brown.
7. Slice to serve.

Chicken Sausage and Broccoli Casserole

Prep time: 10 minutes | Cook time: 20 minutes | Serves 8

- 10 eggs
- 1 cup Cheddar cheese, shredded and divided
- ¾ cup heavy whipping cream
- 1 (12-ounce / 340-g) package cooked chicken sausage
- 1 cup broccoli, chopped
- 2 cloves garlic, minced
- ½ tablespoon salt
- ¼ tablespoon ground black pepper
- Cooking spray

1. Spritz the baking pan with cooking spray.
2. Whisk the eggs with Cheddar and cream in a large bowl to mix well.
3. Combine the cooked sausage, broccoli, garlic, salt, and ground black pepper in a separate bowl. Stir to mix well.
4. Pour the sausage mixture into the baking pan, then spread the egg mixture over to cover.
5. Slide the baking pan into Rack Position 1, select Convection Bake, set temperature to 400°F (205°C) and set time to 20 minutes.
6. When cooking is complete, the egg should be set and a toothpick inserted in the center should come out clean.
7. Serve immediately.

Mediterranean Quiche

Prep time: 10 minutes | Cook time: 30 minutes | Serves 4

- 4 eggs
- ¼ cup chopped Kalamata olives
- ½ cup chopped tomatoes
- ¼ cup chopped onion
- ½ cup milk
- 1 cup crumbled feta cheese
- ½ tablespoon chopped oregano
- ½ tablespoon chopped basil
- Salt and ground black pepper, to taste
- Cooking spray

1. Spritz the baking pan with cooking spray.
2. Whisk the eggs with remaining ingredients in a large bowl. Stir to mix well.
3. Pour the mixture into the prepared baking pan.
4. Slide the baking pan into Rack Position 1, select Convection Bake, set temperature to 340°F (171°C) and set time to 30 minutes.
5. When cooking is complete, the eggs should be set and a toothpick inserted in the center should come out clean.
6. Serve immediately.

Chapter 10
Wraps and Sandwiches

Avocado and Tomato Egg Rolls

Prep time: 10 minutes | Cook time: 5 minutes | Serves 5

- 10 egg roll wrappers
- 3 avocados, peeled and pitted
- 1 tomato, diced
- Salt and ground black pepper, to taste
- Cooking spray

1. Spritz the air fryer basket with cooking spray.
2. Put the tomato and avocados in a food processor. Sprinkle with salt and ground black pepper. Pulse to mix and coarsely mash until smooth.
3. Unfold the wrappers on a clean work surface, then divide the mixture in the center of each wrapper. Roll the wrapper up and press to seal.
4. Transfer the rolls to the pan and spritz with cooking spray.
5. Put the air fryer basket on the baking pan and slide into Rack Position 2, select Air Fry, set temperature to 350ºF (180ºC) and set time to 5 minutes.
6. Flip the rolls halfway through the cooking time.
7. When cooked, the rolls should be golden brown.
8. Serve immediately.

Crispy Crab and Cream Cheese Wontons

Prep time: 10 minutes | Cook time: 10 minutes | Serves 6 to 8

- 24 wonton wrappers, thawed if frozen
- Cooking spray
- Filling:
- 5 ounces (142 g) lump crabmeat, drained and patted dry
- 4 ounces (113 g) cream cheese, at
- room temperature
- 2 scallions, sliced
- 1½ teaspoons toasted sesame oil
- 1 teaspoon Worcestershire sauce
- Kosher salt and ground black pepper, to taste

1. Spritz the air fryer basket with cooking spray.
2. In a medium-size bowl, place all the ingredients for the filling and stir until well mixed. Prepare a small bowl of water alongside.
3. On a clean work surface, lay the wonton wrappers. Scoop 1 teaspoon of the filling in the center of each wrapper. Wet the edges with a touch of water. Fold each wonton wrapper diagonally in half over the filling to form a triangle.
4. Arrange the wontons in the pan. Spritz the wontons with cooking spray.
5. Put the air fryer basket on the baking pan and slide into Rack Position 2, select Air Fry, set temperature to 350ºF (180ºC) and set time to 10 minutes.
6. Flip the wontons halfway through the cooking time.
7. When cooking is complete, the wontons will be crispy and golden brown.
8. Serve immediately.

Cheesy Bacon and Egg Wraps

Prep time: 15 minutes | Cook time: 10 minutes | Serves 3

- 3 corn tortillas
- 3 slices bacon, cut into strips
- 2 scrambled eggs
- 3 tablespoons salsa
- 1 cup grated Pepper Jack cheese
- 3 tablespoons cream cheese, divided
- Cooking spray

1. Spritz the air fryer basket with cooking spray.
2. Unfold the tortillas on a clean work surface, divide the bacon and eggs in the middle of the tortillas, then spread with salsa and scatter with cheeses. Fold the tortillas over.
3. Arrange the tortillas in the pan.
4. Put the air fryer basket on the baking pan and slide into Rack Position 2, select Air Fry, set temperature to 390ºF (199ºC) and set time to 10 minutes.
5. Flip the tortillas halfway through the cooking time.
6. When cooking is complete, the cheeses will be melted and the tortillas will be lightly browned.
7. Serve immediately.

Beef and Bell Pepper Fajitas

Prep time: 15 minutes | Cook time: 10 minutes | Serves 4

- 1 pound (454 g) beef sirloin steak, cut into strips
- 2 shallots, sliced
- 1 orange bell pepper, sliced
- 1 red bell pepper, sliced
- 2 garlic cloves, minced
- 2 tablespoons Cajun seasoning
- 1 tablespoon paprika
- Salt and ground black pepper, to taste
- 4 corn tortillas
- ½ cup shredded Cheddar cheese
- Cooking spray

1. Spritz the air fryer basket with cooking spray.
2. Combine all the ingredients, except for the tortillas and cheese, in a large bowl. Toss to coat well.
3. Pour the beef and vegetables in the pan and spritz with cooking spray.
4. Put the air fryer basket on the baking pan and slide into Rack Position 2, select Air Fry, set temperature to 360ºF (182ºC) and set time to 10 minutes.
5. Stir the beef and vegetables halfway through the cooking time.
6. When cooking is complete, the meat will be browned and the vegetables will be soft and lightly wilted.
7. Unfold the tortillas on a clean work surface and spread the cooked beef and vegetables on top. Scatter with cheese and fold to serve.

Cheesy Potato Taquitos

Prep time: 5 minutes | Cook time: 6 minutes | Makes 12 taquitos

- 2 cups mashed potatoes
- ½ cup shredded Mexican cheese
- 12 corn tortillas
- Cooking spray

1. Line the baking pan with parchment paper.
2. In a bowl, combine the potatoes and cheese until well mixed. Microwave the tortillas on high heat for 30 seconds, or until softened. Add some water to another bowl and set alongside.
3. On a clean work surface, lay the tortillas. Scoop 3 tablespoons of the potato mixture in the center of each tortilla. Roll up tightly and secure with toothpicks if necessary.
4. Arrange the filled tortillas, seam side down, in the prepared baking pan. Spritz the tortillas with cooking spray.
5. Put the air fryer basket on the baking pan and slide into Rack Position 2, select Air Fry, set temperature to 400ºF (205ºC) and set time to 6 minutes.
6. Flip the tortillas halfway through the cooking time.
7. When cooked, the tortillas should be crispy and golden brown.
8. Serve hot.

Chicken and Yogurt Taquitos

Prep time: 15 minutes | Cook time: 12 minutes | Serves 4

- 1 cup cooked chicken, shredded
- ¼ cup Greek yogurt
- ¼ cup salsa
- 1 cup shredded Mozzarella cheese
- Salt and ground black pepper, to taste
- 4 flour tortillas
- Cooking spray

1. Spritz the air fryer basket with cooking spray.
2. Combine all the ingredients, except for the tortillas, in a large bowl. Stir to mix well.
3. Make the taquitos: Unfold the tortillas on a clean work surface, then scoop up 2 tablespoons of the chicken mixture in the middle of each tortilla. Roll the tortillas up to wrap the filling.
4. Arrange the taquitos in the pan and spritz with cooking spray.
5. Put the air fryer basket on the baking pan and slide into Rack Position 2, select Air Fry, set temperature to 380ºF (193ºC) and set time to 12 minutes.
6. Flip the taquitos halfway through the cooking time.
7. When cooked, the taquitos should be golden brown and the cheese should be melted.
8. Serve immediately.

Crispy Chicken Egg Rolls

Prep time: 10 minutes | Cook time: 23 to 24 minutes | Serves 4

- 1 pound (454 g) ground chicken
- 2 teaspoons olive oil
- 2 garlic cloves, minced
- 1 teaspoon grated fresh ginger
- 2 cups white cabbage, shredded
- 1 onion, chopped
- ¼ cup soy sauce
- 8 egg roll wrappers
- 1 egg, beaten
- Cooking spray

1. Spritz the air fryer basket with cooking spray.
2. Heat olive oil in a saucepan over medium heat. Sauté the garlic and ginger in the olive oil for 1 minute, or until fragrant. Add the ground chicken to the saucepan. Sauté for 5 minutes, or until the chicken is cooked through. Add the cabbage, onion and soy sauce and sauté for 5 to 6 minutes, or until the vegetables become soft. Remove the saucepan from the heat.
3. Unfold the egg roll wrappers on a clean work surface. Divide the chicken mixture among the wrappers and brush the edges of the wrappers with the beaten egg. Tightly roll up the egg rolls, enclosing the filling. Arrange the rolls in the pan.
4. Put the air fryer basket on the baking pan and slide into Rack Position 2, select Air Fry, set temperature to 370ºF (188ºC) and set time to 12 minutes.
5. Flip the rolls halfway through the cooking time.
6. When cooked, the rolls will be crispy and golden brown.
7. Transfer to a platter and let cool for 5 minutes before serving.

Air Fried Cream Cheese Wontons

Prep time: 5 minutes | Cook time: 6 minutes | Serves 4

- 2 ounces (57 g) cream cheese, softened
- 1 tablespoon sugar
- 16 square wonton wrappers
- Cooking spray

1. Spritz the air fryer basket with cooking spray.
2. In a mixing bowl, stir together the cream cheese and sugar until well mixed. Prepare a small bowl of water alongside.
3. On a clean work surface, lay the wonton wrappers. Scoop ¼ teaspoon of cream cheese in the center of each wonton wrapper. Dab the water over the wrapper edges. Fold each wonton wrapper diagonally in half over the filling to form a triangle.
4. Arrange the wontons in the pan. Spritz the wontons with cooking spray.
5. Put the air fryer basket on the baking pan and slide into Rack Position 2, select Air Fry, set temperature to 350ºF (180ºC) and set time to 6 minutes.
6. Flip the wontons halfway through the cooking time.
7. When cooking is complete, the wontons will be golden brown and crispy.
8. Divide the wontons among four plates. Let rest for 5 minutes before serving.

Cabbage and Pork Gyoza

Prep time: 10 minutes | Cook time: 10 minutes | Makes 48 gyozas

- 1 pound (454 g) ground pork
- 1 head Napa cabbage (about 1 pound / 454 g), sliced thinly and minced
- ½ cup minced scallions
- 1 teaspoon minced fresh chives
- 1 teaspoon soy sauce
- 1 teaspoon minced fresh ginger
- 1 tablespoon minced garlic
- 1 teaspoon granulated sugar
- 2 teaspoons kosher salt
- 48 to 50 wonton or dumpling wrappers
- Cooking spray

1. Spritz the air fryer basket with cooking spray. Set aside.
2. Make the filling: Combine all the ingredients, except for the wrappers in a large bowl. Stir to mix well.
3. Unfold a wrapper on a clean work surface, then dab the edges with a little water. Scoop up 2 teaspoons of the filling mixture in the center.
4. Make the gyoza: Fold the wrapper over to filling and press the edges to seal. Pleat the edges if desired. Repeat with remaining wrappers and fillings.
5. Arrange the gyozas in the pan and spritz with cooking spray.
6. Put the air fryer basket on the baking pan and slide into Rack Position 2, select Air Fry, set temperature to 360ºF (182ºC) and set time to 10 minutes.
7. Flip the gyozas halfway through the cooking time.
8. When cooked, the gyozas will be golden brown.
9. Serve immediately.

Sweet Potato and Black Bean Burritos

Prep time: 15 minutes | Cook time: 30 minutes | Makes 6 burritos

- 2 sweet potatoes, peeled and cut into a small dice
- 1 tablespoon vegetable oil
- Kosher salt and ground black pepper, to taste
- 6 large flour tortillas
- 1 (16-ounce / 454-g) can refried black beans, divided
- 1½ cups baby spinach, divided
- 6 eggs, scrambled
- ¾ cup grated Cheddar cheese, divided
- ¼ cup salsa
- ¼ cup sour cream
- Cooking spray

1. Put the sweet potatoes in a large bowl, then drizzle with vegetable oil and sprinkle with salt and black pepper. Toss to coat well.
2. Place the potatoes in the air fryer basket.
3. Put the air fryer basket on the baking pan and slide into Rack Position 2, select Air Fry, set temperature to 400ºF (205ºC) and set time to 10 minutes.
4. Flip the potatoes halfway through the cooking time.
5. When done, the potatoes should be lightly browned. Remove the potatoes from the oven.
6. Unfold the tortillas on a clean work surface. Divide the black beans, spinach, air fried sweet potatoes, scrambled eggs, and cheese on top of the tortillas.
7. Fold the long side of the tortillas over the filling, then fold in the shorter side to wrap the filling to make the burritos.
8. Wrap the burritos in the aluminum foil and put in the pan.
9. Put the air fryer basket on the baking pan and slide into Rack Position 2, select Air Fry, set temperature to 350ºF (180ºC) and set time to 20 minutes.
10. Flip the burritos halfway through the cooking time.
11. Remove the burritos from the oven and spread with sour cream and salsa. Serve immediately.

Appendix 1: Measurement Conversion Chart

VOLUME EQUIVALENTS(DRY)

US STANDARD	METRIC (APPROXIMATE)
1/8 teaspoon	0.5 mL
1/4 teaspoon	1 mL
1/2 teaspoon	2 mL
3/4 teaspoon	4 mL
1 teaspoon	5 mL
1 tablespoon	15 mL
1/4 cup	59 mL
1/2 cup	118 mL
3/4 cup	177 mL
1 cup	235 mL
2 cups	475 mL
3 cups	700 mL
4 cups	1 L

VOLUME EQUIVALENTS(LIQUID)

US STANDARD	US STANDARD (OUNCES)	METRIC (APPROXIMATE)
2 tablespoons	1 fl.oz.	30 mL
1/4 cup	2 fl.oz.	60 mL
1/2 cup	4 fl.oz.	120 mL
1 cup	8 fl.oz.	240 mL
1 1/2 cup	12 fl.oz.	355 mL
2 cups or 1 pint	16 fl.oz.	475 mL
4 cups or 1 quart	32 fl.oz.	1 L
1 gallon	128 fl.oz.	4 L

TEMPERATURES EQUIVALENTS

FAHRENHEIT(F)	CELSIUS(C) (APPROXIMATE)
225 °F	107 °C
250 °F	120 °C
275 °F	135 °C
300 °F	150 °C
325 °F	160 °C
350 °F	180 °C
375 °F	190 °C
400 °F	205 °C
425 °F	220 °C
450 °F	235 °C
475 °F	245 °C
500 °F	260 °C

WEIGHT EQUIVALENTS

US STANDARD	METRIC (APPROXIMATE)
1 ounce	28 g
2 ounces	57 g
5 ounces	142 g
10 ounces	284 g
15 ounces	425 g
16 ounces (1 pound)	455 g
1.5 pounds	680 g
2 pounds	907 g

Appendix 2: Recipe index

Made in the USA
Middletown, DE
29 November 2020